IMPRISON HIM!

IMPRISON HIM!

BY
MIRIAM WOOD

PACIFIC PRESS PUBLISHING ASSOCIATION
Mountain View, California
Omaha, Nebraska
Oshawa, Ontario

Cover illustration and book design by Dale Rusch
Copyright © 1980 by
Pacific Press Publishing Association
Litho in United States of America
All Rights Reserved

Library of Congress Catalog Card No. 79-90083
ISBN No. 0-8163-0354-1

Dedication

To all who, through the ages,
have suffered for God.

"As the Father hath sent me,
So send I you."

So send I you to labor unrewarded,
To serve unpaid, unloved, unsought, unknown,
To bear rebuke, to suffer scorn and scoffing—
So send I you to toil for me alone.

So send I you to loneliness and longing,
With heart ahung'ring for the loved and known,
Forsaking home and kindred, friend and dear one—
So send I you to know my love alone.

So send I you to leave your life's ambition,
To die to dear desire, self-will resign.
To labor long and love where men revile you;
So send I you to lose your life in mine.

So send I you to hearts made hard by hatred,
To eyes made blind because they will not see,
To spend, tho it be blood— to spend and spare not—
So send I you to taste of Calvary

"As the Father hath sent me,
So send I you."

Prologue

This is a true story. All the incidents related actually took place. However, the names have been changed; there is no "Antonio Silva" or "Elena" or "Maria" or "Lucila." These are pseudonyms for the four people who lived this experience.

I first heard the story in 1978 when I was visiting South America. My husband and I were guests in the home of one of the young couples staffing a union mission. Present at the dinner table was another guest, who had arrived only that day to take over the presidency of the mission.

Someone whispered to me, "He is one of the pastors who was imprisoned in ————." Fascinated, as we all are on meeting extraordinary people who have suffered and prevailed over awesome circumstances, I watched him closely. Handsome, tall, dark-haired, and dark-eyed, but more. He seemed to be attuned to all the suffering and sadness of the universe.

As our meal progressed, I timidly asked him if he would mind telling a few things about his ordeal. I realize now that though he was reluctant to relive even briefly the horror of the experience, his courtesy would not permit him to refuse a request, particularly from a visitor from another country. And so he talked, and we listened with ever-growing attention. Slowly the conviction grew that Seventh-day Adventists everywhere must also share the suffering that he and his wife and children had endured so heroically.

When he had finished a brief version of his story, I exclaimed, "Please let me write a book about this!"

He was reluctant. "Others might be harmed if all the facts were made public," he replied.

"Then we won't make them public," I assured him. "We won't mention your name or the names of your family, and we will not mention the specific country where this took place."

He thought carefully for a few moments and conceded: "On that basis I will try to get the material to you after you return to the United States." And in spite of his heavy responsibilities in assuming the leadership of a difficult mission he somehow found the time to share his story with me in a form that made the writing of this book possible.

A number of points must be kept in mind. First, while there were four Seventh-day Adventists thrown into the prison, two of them Brazilian pastors, in addition to a national pastor and a national colporteur (who was imprisoned before the others), I have undertaken to tell only the story of "Pastor Silva." Obviously other books could be written featuring each of the three companions. I have not met these other men, I am sorry to say. My focal point is "Antonio Silva."

Also, in the country where this outrage took place, religious people of all faiths are still being imprisoned, still being persecuted. With this in mind I have deliberately "blurred" certain situations and incidents for the protection of these helpless believers. At no time do I mention the specific steps taken to secure Pastor Silva's release, for the reasons that I have outlined.

Probably the largest hurdle to overcome has been the reluctance of the "Silvas" to be depicted as I see them—magnificent Christians, full of faith and courage, whose valor through a nightmare of suffering and terror stands as an inspiration and a beacon light to every Christian. They do not regard themselves as special or unique. They are unusually modest and self-effacing Christians. Nonetheless, they have contributed a chapter to a modern "Acts of the Apostles"—a story that must be preserved in our church chronicles.

Probably every Christian has asked himself from time to time what he would do if he were called upon to suffer for his faith. "Antonio and Elena Silva" have answered that question. They or others need never have any doubts as to the strength of their commitment.

Writing this book, vicariously sharing the shattering experiences of "Antonio" and "Elena," has been a deeply moving experience for me. My hope and prayer is that those who read will also resolve to remain true to God no matter what the cost.

Miriam Wood

8

Contents

Beginnings and Foreshadowings

The guard opened the cell door and, with a hand sign that expected no argument, motioned Pastor Silva inside. With an echoing clang the guard slammed the door from the outside and turned the key with awful finality. As though from a great distance, he heard a chorus of "SCORE!" from many throats. Dazed, unbelieving, disoriented, Pastor Antonio Silva gazed around at the packed humanity crowded into the small room. Some were standing, others attempting to sit, still others, obviously ill, begging for a small space in which to lie.

In the late-evening dusk two small bulbs in the high-ceilinged room gave light so weak that the prisoners seemed almost like shadows. In Pastor Silva's ears sounds that would be his constant companion for nearly six months began to register—sounds that he would never forget: the despairing cries of hopeless men snatched from their families, hungry men, sick men, men whose minds had snapped from terror, men who had lost contact with the real world.

Turning to his companions who had been thrown into the cell with him, he gasped, "We must pray. Oh, God, please help us now!"

As they prayed, the thought came to Pastor Silva that it was Friday night. Why wasn't he in his clean and comfortable apartment, sharing the joy of greeting the Sabbath with the three people dearest in the world to him? Would he never see Elena, his beloved wife, and his two little girls, Maria and Lucila, again?

But even the comfort of repeating those precious names was denied him. "Go wash yourselves! Go wash yourselves!" shouted a group of prisoners.

In his shock and confusion the words made no sense to him. What were they talking about? Why should he wash? He was clean, immaculately clean, as he always was. They must be mocking him, making some ghoulish joke.

One of his companions began to understand. "They're telling us that we have to go over in that corner and scrub ourselves," he explained. And so the three of them pressed their way through the tightly packed mass of inmates who squeezed themselves even closer to allow the new prisoners to reach the washing place.

Later, Pastor Silva learned that many prisoners were brought into the cell filthy and diseased. Because avoiding close physical contact was impossible, and realizing that even their sanity depended upon some kind of organization, the prisoners had chosen several men to establish whatever rules could be maintained. Pastor Silva could not know on this terrible Friday night that as the weeks and months would pass, he would be profoundly grateful for this simple hygienic precaution and for similar rules.

But now he became aware of a general movement, a surge, as groups of the prisoners began to drop to the floor. He watched them position themselves on their sides with their arms pressed tightly to their bodies. He realized that it was time to sleep. Sleep? Had it not been so tragic, it might almost have been amusing. How could this seething mass of humanity, packed like peaches in a jar, sleep? However, overwhelming fatigue soon engulfed him. The long day of questioning, the shock of his imprisonment, the horror of his present situation—all engulfed him. Turning to Pastors C. and M., he said, "We must try to lie down as best we can, impossible though it seems."

Removing his coat, he spread it on a small patch of floor; his shoes became his pillow. For a fleeting moment he thought of Jacob, so long ago, with the stone under his head. Though physical exhaustion made him half sick, sleep seemed as foreign as the world now lost to him. He shut his eyes and began to pray silently:

"Oh, Lord, please protect us here in this terrible place; watch over us and influence the authorities to release us. But more than that, please watch over our dear, beloved ones at home and let no evil come to them. But most of all, Lord, make us able to accept Thy will no matter what it is."

With that prayer came a measure of peace.

But then Pastor Silva became aware of insistent stinging sensations all over his body—and with a sinking heart he realized that the prison cell was literally alive with lice. His aching body twisted and writhed in the small space. As the night wore on, some prisoners talked, some screamed in frustration, and a few slept. Above were those tiny light bulbs with their eerie glow.

Why am I here? How did it all begin? These questions beat against Pastor Silva's brain over and over. Why was he in a strange country, in a hostile land, as the president of a mission where the news of Christ's salvation was so needed? As the hours dragged, his restless mind went back to the beginning of it all—to the decision to accept mission service which had led to this terror.

"June 22, 1971—I wonder how I remember that date so clearly?" he asked himself. Back he went to that day of Ingathering along the streets of Joinville in the state of Santa Catarina, Brazil. For a year and a half he had been a mission president in this area of South Brazil. He loved his work. His plans and his hopes for the future were high. As he walked along the street, between business establishments which he was contacting, his heart was so full of the joy of Christian service that he almost felt like singing. He appreciated this beautiful little city with many German immigrants, who had made it a clean and prosperous place.

"Pastor Silva! Pastor Silva!" Turning, he saw one of his local ministers hurrying down the sidewalk.

"The local telephone station got in touch with me to say that they have a message for you from our union president. He wants you to phone him back at union headquarters as soon as possible," the local minister told him.

After thanking his friend, Pastor Silva felt a flicker of anxiety pass through his mind. Could there be something wrong with Elena or the two little girls? Probably not, he decided, for the union president would have made that clear. No, it had to be something else. Perhaps there was a call for one of Pastor Silva's workers to join another conference or mission. Yes, that must be it.

Since the shops would soon close, he decided that he would finish his few remaining calls and eat a light meal before making his telephone call. In this somewhat isolated area of Brazil a long-distance call was a rather formidable undertaking. Pastor Silva, a veteran of such experiences, settled himself for the customary frustrations; but to his surprise, the connection was made almost immediately.

Hardly taking time to make the customary polite inquiries about Pastor Silva's health or the progress of the Ingathering, the union president announced, "I have a very serious matter to place before you. In my hands at this moment is a call for you to go to Africa as a mission president in ———!''

Pastor Silva's reaction was one of amusement. His union president was a great and good human being—who very much enjoyed a small joke with his workers; in fact, he could joke with a perfectly straight face. Only real mental agility enabled one to keep up with him. Considering this, Pastor Silva replied, ''Now isn't that interesting! I wonder how they ever found me down here in this little corner of Brazil. Well, I guess it really is the age of miracles.''

Then, pausing for a moment, he asked, ''Pastor A———, what is it that you really want to talk to me about?''

''No, no,'' the president insisted. ''This is not a joke—there really is a call. The need of the mission is extreme, and after much prayer and thought the mission board feels that you are the man to meet that need.''

Now shaken and uneasy, Pastor Silva replied, ''I've never known you to carry a joke this far before, Pastor.''

Almost harshly the union president answered, ''I was never more serious in my life. The call is here, and I thought you should know it as soon as possible, though we will not bring it up officially until our next union committee meeting.''

Lying in the prison cell, twisting and turning, his body aching, Pastor Silva could remember, as clearly as though it had just happened, the strange air of unreality that the little telephone building had assumed. The union president went on talking. Pastor Silva was dazed. His Brazilian duties, which he loved and which he thought would progress in an orderly course, were suddenly upset by a psychological earthquake.

The union president continued, ''Pastor Silva, the last thing in the world we want is for you to go. You are doing a wonderful work here in this union. You have a very special way with the people, and the Lord is blessing you abundantly. If I were being selfish, I would say that we need you every bit as much here as they need you in Africa. Please remember that as you pray about this.''

Pastor Silva stood in the little telephone building holding the receiver in his hand long after his union president had said his good-byes and hung up. Had this really happened? Was it a dream? Never in his life had he considered the possibility of mission service; somehow, this had never become part of his lifelong commitment to the gospel ministry.

Walking back to his hotel, mechanically crossing the well-groomed streets, he thought to himself, "Well, receiving a call doesn't mean that I must go. The Lord gives us the power of choice. I can serve Him just as well here as in Africa. And Pastor A. has assured me that I really am very much needed. They can call someone else—"

But the moment the words crossed his mind, he breathed a prayer for forgiveness. He must not deny his Lord by asking that someone else take his place—if the Lord clearly indicated that it *was* his place. But was Africa to be "his" place? How could it be? So many things had to be considered. After preparing for bed he knelt and prayed earnestly for guidance and for peace. Neither would come. Tossing and turning, he was glad to see the first light of dawn.

Yet, in spite of his churning mind, he faced two more days of Ingathering. He felt a great need to confide in someone, to share his misgivings. A very private man, Pastor Silva wasn't in the habit of discussing his innermost feelings with colleagues. To phone his wife and break this astonishing news to her in that way was unthinkable. As his need to talk to another human being became intense, he called aside his Ingathering companion, the conference youth director, and informed him of the call to Africa.

His youth director was as shocked as Pastor Silva had been. "But you haven't been our president in this mission very long!" he protested. "You have so many wonderful programs going. The work is progressing in a way it never has before in this area. We just can't spare you. God wants you here. I beg of you, please don't go!"

Even as the comfort of those words which he so much wanted to hear swept over him, Pastor Silva was ashamed. "Forgive me, Lord," he prayed silently. "Thou knowest that this call is not what I had planned for my life, but please make me willing to fit into *Thy* plans, whatever they are."

During the three-hour bus ride back home to Florianopólis, the emotional and mental battle continued. Could he ask Elena to leave their home, their family, and their friends, and go to a country beset with political turmoil? As he thought of Elena, a small half-smile played about his lips. What a woman she was! What a wife! Strong, glowing, full of optimism and courage, she was special. He had asked himself many times through their years together how he could have been so fortunate as to find this woman to share his life. The daughter of a minister, she had been bred and nurtured in the crucible of service, and in the belief that God's message of salvation must be carried to the world. No, he need not worry about Elena's willingness to go with him—it was his own willingness that he must consider.

Little Maria, ten, and Lucila, eight, had captivated his heart since birth and now occupied a large part of his dreams for the future. One aspect he enjoyed most about his present life was that his home was only about twenty meters from the mission office. As Elena went about her daily work, usually singing softly to herself, she could glance from her window to Antonio's office window and send him a silent message of love. In the nearby schoolyard she could watch her two girls playing with their friends during recess periods.

Pastor Silva thought, with a sudden catch in his throat, of a little custom he and Elena had. Once in a while, when especially rushed, if he needed something he had left at home, he would go to his office window and give a long, low whistle that would bring Elena to her window.

"What do you need, love?" she would ask, and then she would bring whatever he requested.

"The love between us has always been so special," he thought to himself. "We haven't had the cross words and misunderstandings that mar so many marriages. We're still sweethearts. We're so happy. Will I endanger all that if I ask Elena to go to a strange country? Will there be a school for our little girls? Would we have a place to live in that we could make into a home?"

He resolved to put the conflict out of his mind for at least a few hours and enjoy his homecoming. Elena and Maria and Lucila always welcomed him eagerly, even if his absence had been for only a few days. Flinging open the door, he called, "Hello! I'm home!" The **three of them came running, as always. He hugged and kissed each** one of them in turn. The little home had never looked so lovely. The floors glistened; the simple furniture shone with Elena's good care. And he had almost forgotten how pretty the blue sofa was—the sofa they had saved for so long and had just bought. Each piece of furniture represented real planning and sacrifice, for his minister's salary wasn't large enough to make great purchases. They had bought their furniture one piece at a time. He almost smiled to himself as he realized that a king certainly wouldn't consider this a palace, but in its clean and shining simplicity it represented all he had ever dreamed of.

The two little girls ran back outdoors to their play; and Pastor Silva bustled about, unpacking, making conversation, trying to hide his **concern. But it didn't work.**

"What is it, Antonio? Is something wrong?" she asked, placing her hand gently on his arm, her loving face full of concern.

He was silent for a moment. Then he put his arms about her, and they stood there in the cozy room, just the two of them, in the quietness.

"Let me take my bath; then we'll talk," he promised her.

The hot water and fragrant soap cleansed and soothed his body; Elena often teased him gently about his love for being always immaculately clean and tidy. "Cleanliness is next to godliness," he always said, smiling.

Then the news could be postponed no longer.

"Let's sit together on our new blue couch," he suggested; and as they sat there hand in hand, he told her what had happened.

At first she was as startled as he had been.

"But what—what about school for the girls—what about . . . " Her questions went on until he placed his hand gently over her lips.

"I don't know the answer to any of those questions, dearest one," he told her. "But God knows them. Let's kneel down right now and pray that He will be very near to us at this time."

As they poured out their hearts there by the blue couch, a feeling of peace settled over them. For the first time since the telephone call Pastor Silva's heart was at rest. God had led him throughout his lifetime and would continue to lead him.

Elena's face was beautiful and glowing when they arose from their knees.

"Whatever God wants us to do, that is what we will do," she told him. "I can make a home anywhere. But the decision must be yours. Wherever you go, I will go. As long as we have each other and the little girls, we will be happy. If the Lord is calling you to Africa, then He has a special work for you to do there."

Dear Elena! Had he ever had a moment's doubt that this is how she would feel? They decided not to tell the children just yet, however. Children need security and tranquillity. They need to live in their own small, happy world, untroubled by adult problems.

In spite of the peace they had felt after their prayer, Antonio and Elena did not yet hear a clear and ringing Yes or No. How, then, could the issue be resolved?

"First of all, the call must be passed by the union committee. Let's leave ourselves in their hands. It is possible that they will not pass the call along to us," Pastor Silva said almost wistfully.

17

But after prayer and careful consideration the union committee felt that they could not deny the needs of the mission field. The official call was put into Pastor Silva's hands. Now the decision must be made. Maria and Lucila must be told of the situation; for it would be unfair if they were to hear of it from their friends, who themselves might have overheard conversation in their homes.

Again Pastor Silva called the little family to the pretty living room, and this time all four of them sat on the blue couch.

"Girls," he said quietly, "something has happened in our family that we never expected. I have been asked to go to Africa and become one of the mission presidents."

Four eyes flew wide open.

"Africa!" exclaimed Maria. "But we wouldn't be able to talk to anybody! Don't they speak African in Africa?"

Pastor and Mrs. Silva smiled at their little daughter.

"Not in the country they've asked us to go to," Pastor Silva told her. "In this particular country they speak Portuguese. That's one of the reasons the church wants me to go and take charge of the work there."

Of course the little girls were full of childish questions, but their trust and faith in their parents were so complete that they didn't appear to be in the least upset. After they had gone back to their play, Antonio turned to Elena.

"Perhaps a little child shall lead them," he quoted softly.

Though he hadn't said too much about it, one of the strongest heartaches Pastor Silva faced at the thought of a move to Africa was leaving his elderly, very feeble parents, who had already suffered much sorrow and tragedy in their lifetime. After all that had happened to them, how could he say to these two fragile loved ones, "I am going across the sea to a strange land. You are old. I will be in dangerous places. I may never see you again"?

Sitting at his desk, with the soft Brazilian breeze blowing fragrantly through the room, Pastor Silva thought of the stories that his father had told him from childhood.

Father Silva had been born in Russia, of Dutch descent. When he was seventeen, he heard the Adventist message and accepted it fully and gladly, though he was not baptized until he was twenty-four. The girl who became his wife, also Russian Dutch, had been reared in the Adventist faith; the two of them had married somewhat late in life, when Father Silva was nearly thirty. Both families had a strong

18

Mennonite background. Faith in God was a part of the warp and woof of their entire existence.

The couple moved to Siberia, where life seemed peaceful though hard in that cold, underdeveloped, and barren land. Father Silva, the local church elder, often translated sermons by German pastors who were sent to the area, since he spoke German as well as Russian. But everything changed in 1918 with the coming of the Russian revolution. Religion was outlawed. Those who refused to give up their faith were relentlessly pursued and persecuted, tortured and murdered.

Even in the warmth and security of his office Pastor Silva shuddered as he remembered the stories of what it had been like.

"We managed to exist in Siberia until 1930," his father had told him. "But then we knew that not one of us would survive if we did not somehow move to another country. We had so little money. And it took a long time to find people who would help us at the risk of their own lives. We had two children then, Peter and Johanna. I could not let them be brought up to hate God, and I could not let them be killed. So we started out."

At this point in the story Father Silva always had to fight for self-control. "While we were crossing Germany, our precious little Johanna died," he would finally say quietly.

"Though it had cost Johanna's life, we had to go on, even with the risk. So many of our relatives had already been taken to the work camps and had died of overwork, exposure, and torture. We knew that we would be next. All of them were wonderful, law-abiding, Christian people. The only crime they had committed was that they refused to give up their faith in God. They were Adventists and Mennonites and Baptists."

Father and Mother Silva finally arrived in Brazil and started a new life. Here Antonio was born, growing up as a Portuguese-speaking Brazilian. Financially, life had been very, very hard in this new land; but the freedom to worship God in peace meant everything to the family.

With this background of suffering, could Antonio tell his parents that he was contemplating mission service in a country which might soon be taken over by the same kind of government which had murdered most of his relatives, exiled his parents, and caused the death of his sister? Did he have the right to subject them to this strain in their old age?

"We must go to see Father and Mother and put the whole matter before them at once,'' he told Elena as soon as the official call came. He knew that he had been postponing the visit, dreading the hurt he might inflict.

As always, Father and Mother Silva were waiting at the door of their little home to hug the two little girls, whom Elena had dressed in their prettiest little dresses. The old couple's pleasure in the children was never-ending. They cherished each visit, wishing that it were possible to be with the children all the time, yet never interfering with Antonio's and Elena's lives.

After all the greetings and the inquiries about Antonio's work were over—the latter being of the keenest interest to Father Silva—the moment of truth could be postponed no longer. Antonio sat down beside his aging father. "Father," he said, "I don't know how to tell you this, but I have received a call to go to a country in Africa to be the president of the mission there. They tell me that I am badly needed."

His father gazed wordlessly back at him. Antonio hurried on, his heart aching. "But it seems to me, seeing you and Mother so frail, and knowing that the years are moving along, that I must refuse to go. It would be so hard for me to separate from you after all you have lived through and then to be so far away that you could not rely on me if you needed something."

Still his father was silent.

"And Father—we might never see one another again."

At that point Antonio got one of the biggest surprises of his life. His old and feeble father stood up, slowly straightened himself to his full height and, with his dark brown eyes flashing, roared, "BUT—BUT—why do you say to me 'BUT'? If God is calling you, then that is where you must go!"

Antonio leaped to his feet and threw his arms around the old patriarch. "Father, I haven't heard that tone in your voice since I was a little boy and got into mischief." He choked between laughter and tears.

Father Silva patted Antonio's shoulder, his own eyes moist.

"My dear, dear son," he replied quietly, "you must not let your mother and me stand in the way of God's call. We are old, it is true. And it is true that perhaps we may never see you again. Hardest of all will be to give up being with the little girls." Here his voice broke for a moment. Then he went on. "But we have lived our lives, and we have a certain and sure hope of a better land, where we can all be together forever—even our dear ones who suffered and died in Russia. Our precious Johanna will be with us. If you can hasten Christ's coming by mission service, then that is what God wants and what I want for you.''

So the question was answered. But what would Elena's parents say?

''Now that we know how my dear mother and father feel, we must visit your parents immediately,'' Antonio told Elena. ''We must talk to them face to face. I know how much they love you, and I don't want them to think that I would make a decision like this unless you were fully agreed and unless they had been consulted.''

Elena's parents lived about 120 kilometers from São Paulo. The little girls were delighted with the trip in the new Volkswagen—well, it was almost new, since they had had the little car only a scant two years. The four of them talked, sang songs, and played games as they drove along. Pastor Silva's heart was very full of the joy of his family, the joy of his work, the beauty of having found something to which to dedicate his life. The countryside had never before seemed so beautiful. Home had never seemed so precious.

Of course the first item on the agenda after their arrival was a delicious meal which Elena's mother had ready for them. Then they had to catch up on all the family news, on all the things which had happened since last they were together. But Antonio couldn't enter into all this happy talk quite as enthusiastically as he normally did. Squaring his shoulders, he determined to bring the problem out into the open at once.

''Mother and Father, could we all go into the living room?'' he asked.

Puzzled, they agreed. The little girls started to run outdoors.

''Maria and Lucila, I'd like you to stay with us for just a little while,'' he told them gently. ''You're getting to be big girls. You need to take your places in the family circle.''

Their eyes big and round, the little girls followed the adults into the cheerful living room, wondering what was about to happen. Elena's father and mother glanced at each other uneasily. Was something wrong?

Pastor Silva broke the silence. ''Mother and Father,'' he announced softly, ''I have been called to a country in Africa to take charge of the work there—a country where Portuguese is the language.''

Never was silence more thunderous. His parents-in-law were trying to grasp in an instant the significance of what he had said. In one moment the serenity and security of their lives had been changed forever. Sensing their confusion, Pastor Silva went on gently.

"I'd like to tell you all about my early life," he said. "Some of it you know, but Maria and Lucila have heard very little of it, for they are only now big enough to understand. Everyone needs to know about the past so that he can understand what kind of influences made him what he is."

Maria clapped her hands. "You're going to tell us a story, aren't you, Daddy?"

He smiled at the pretty child. "Yes, it is a story; but it's a true one, and it's about your daddy."

Then he began. "You know that my family was born and lived in Russia and Siberia and immigrated to Brazil in 1930, after years of great suffering because of their belief in God. But now let me tell you how things were for my parents when they finally reached Brazil. When they had lived here only a few years, I was born in the state of Santa Catarina. I can remember being five years old and being very, very poor. My father lost all he had in Europe. He had to start all over again, doing what he could to earn enough for us to have a roof over our heads and very simple food.

"There was no money to buy clothes. My mother made everything we wore, out of old discarded clothes and scraps of material. She took my father's clothes, when they were too shabby for him to wear longer, and made them over for me."

Lucila jumped up and looked straight into her father's eyes, surprised. She had never imagined that he had been as poorly dressed as those sad little boys she had seen on the streets.

"That's not the worst thing that can happen to a person, dear," he comforted her. She cuddled down beside him as he continued.

"I remember one day Mother was making a little suit for me—at least it had trousers and a coat—and she wanted me to come in from my play and try it on. At first I didn't want to stop what I was doing—and it's so long ago that I can't even remember what it was, so don't ask me, girls!—but when I finally got the suit on, I looked down at myself for a long time."

Interrupting, Maria asked, "Why didn't you look in the mirror, Daddy?"

"We didn't have a full-length mirror," he told her. "We had just a little hand mirror."

22

Thinking back on those hard days, he was silent for a moment. Then he went on. "As I looked at the suit, an idea struck me. I turned to my mother. 'Mother,' I said, 'I look just like a pastor in this suit, don't I?'

"My father was a local church elder and very active in the church work. It was really his life. Suddenly I realized that more than anything else in the world I wanted to be a pastor.

"Mother couldn't help laughing, though, for here I was only five years old and wondering if I already looked like a pastor!

"But as the years passed by, it began to seem as though I could never realize that ambition. When I was seven, my parents enrolled me in a public primary school near our home. The Adventist school was so far away they feared I couldn't manage the long walk twice a day. But as they became aware of what I was learning, they were troubled. They had left their homeland because of their religious beliefs, and they wanted me to have the same firm grounding in truth which they had.

"When it was time for the second school year to begin, Father called me to him.

" 'Son,' he asked, 'do you think you could walk the eight kilometers back and forth each day to the Adventist school?'

" 'Of course I can!' I exclaimed. Boys like to think there's nothing they can't do, you know."

Maria interrupted. "Well, I think a girl could walk that far, too!"

Pastor Silva smiled. "Of course she could, especially if her name happened to be Maria."

Satisfied, she sank back as her father continued.

"But the distance wasn't the only problem. In order to keep the school running tuition had to be charged, but we had absolutely no money to pay it. My father wouldn't have asked a favor for himself, but he was so determined for me to have a Christian education that he humbled himself and asked the teacher if I could attend free of charge, with the understanding that later on, if our finances improved, he would pay all he owed.

"The teacher agreed, and so every year until I was eleven I walked the eight kilometers, in rain and shine. And even when I was sick I tried to go, because I felt it was such a privilege to attend that school.

"When I had finished the four primary grades I was nearly twelve. Oh, how I wanted to keep going to school! There was nothing I loved more than learning. But things were getting worse with our family finances. During World War II everything was upset, and our little family just couldn't get enough to eat with what my father was earning. So I began to go throughout the neighborhood, asking for little odd jobs in order to earn money to help my mother buy food. As I got older, I was able to get better jobs. It was so satisfying to me to see the look of worry and strain gradually lifting from my parents' faces because of the money I was able to bring them.''

Elena felt her eyes misting over as she thought of the brave, quiet boy, giving up his life's ambitions so gladly, and giving up a carefree childhood and youth.

"But when I was about seventeen, I suddenly thought, 'Why, I could study at night. I could enroll in the night classes at one of the schools in town, and even though I couldn't take many subjects at one time, at least I would be learning something.'

"And that's what I did. I would work all day—I had already bought an old bicycle that I rode into town each day—and then I would ride back home to eat my supper; then ride back into town for my classes. It was always about eleven p.m. when I got home. I really developed strong legs from all that bicycle riding.''

Lucila tugged at his arm. "But Daddy," she asked, "why didn't you ride the bus?"

Softly he replied, "There wasn't money enough for that—and we lived so far out there wasn't even a bus, little one.''

There, with his wife and little daughters and his mother- and father-in-law, Pastor Silva had to pause for a moment to struggle with his emotions as he remembered how it had been when it seemed as though his life's ambitions would never be realized. He continued softly.

"Late at night, when I would get home from school, I used to go into our yard out under the stars. We had no electricity in our house, so the only light came down from God's heaven. I used to kneel down and open my heart to the Lord, asking Him to give me power to overcome the daily temptations I faced as a young man in my job. Then I would pray earnestly that somehow, someway, someday, I could go to college and study to become a minister. From the human viewpoint, it seemed impossible, but all things are possible with God. For four long years I knelt in the dark yard nearly every night, praying the same prayer. By then I was twenty-two, but by keeping at my night classes I had finished the first part of the secondary school level. Now it seemed to me that I just *must* go to an Adventist college.

Things were better for my parents financially. But I had no money to pay tuition.

"My mother knew of my strong desire to be a minister. She said to me, 'My dear son, you have always been completely faithful in tithing your money, just as I taught you when you were a little boy. You have been faithful and true to God in your conduct. I know that He has many ways to make a college education possible for you. Let's pray that He will open the door.'

"God did open the door—the door to the canvassing work. In just two and a half months I had earned enough money to be admitted to the Adventist college in São Paulo. Of course at age twenty-two I still had to finish my secondary studies and then embark on the four-year theology course. But God led me each step of the way. I canvassed in the summers, did without many things, and by the time I was twenty-five I was in the first year of the theological course. It was a dream come true."

Then he paused and looked across the room at Elena.

"But that wasn't the only dream which came true. The most wonderful dream was meeting the girl who became my wife and your mother, Maria and Lucila."

Both the little girls jumped to their feet.

"Oh, Daddy, tell us about when you met Mommy, and what happened, and—well, everything!" they urged.

But Pastor Silva felt that he'd talked long enough and said all that needed to be said just then.

"I can tell you the rest at another time, girls, and that will give you something to look forward to. But for now, I want Grandmother and Grandfather to know that I have always felt that the Lord had a plan for my life—a plan that I should be a minister in spite of the poverty. I have loved every day I have spent in His service. If God is now calling me to a strange land, I don't want to deny His call."

He paused for a moment. Tears formed in his eyes and rolled slowly down his cheeks.

With difficulty, through the lump in his throat, he whispered, "I *cannot* deny God's call."

The eyes of the two little girls opened wide with surprise. Their strong father—weeping?

Elena, sitting beside him, spoke instantly.

"Though I will miss both of you so desperately, dearest Mother and Father, I am willing to go with Antonio. I also love my work as his wife and his helpmeet; I can't imagine any other kind of life.''

Though struggling in their hearts as Antonio talked, now Elena's parents could also say to the young couple, ''You must go where God leads.''

As he thought back on that day, with the sounds and the smells of the prison cell around him, Pastor Silva remembered the tears that had been shed by all of them at the end of the talk. He wondered if his little girls would remember what he had said about how much being a worker for God meant to him. If he never saw them again, would that talk have a lasting effect on their lives? Would they, too, serve God with all their hearts?

But then his mind went back again to the happy, busy days of preparing to leave Brazil—those days with Elena's parents, his parents, the good meals, the visits with aunts and uncles, the picnics. Time passes so quickly when joy is present.

Then the time came to sell their household goods—the treasured things they had bought when he and Elena were married and those added during the years. How hard it had been to part with each piece of simple furniture, plain as it was! The scratches on some of the chairs, put there by small baby hands and toys when unsteady feet were learning to walk, brought back a flood of memories. And the new blue sofa. (Twisting and turning on the dirty cell floor, Pastor Silva thought to himself, ''How can I even remember a thing like a couch at a time like this?'' Yet it seemed to represent all the warmth and security and love that had been the very center of his life.)

Passports and other documents came through. The last box to be shipped was packed. The suitcases which the four of them would carry on the plane were ready. Now there remained only a final trip through various parts of Brazil for a final good-bye to their dear ones. They tried to say everything—but much was left unsaid. Hearts were full.

And suddenly, very early in the morning of May 18, they were at the São Paulo airport. Remembering, Pastor Silva could feel again the tightness in his stomach, the nervousness, the excitement of the little girls, the brave sadness of his father's face. His mother had not been physically able to face the ordeal of the airport good-byes. He'd told her a loving and private good-bye. Dear, dear Mother, with all her patient sewing for him in his childhood, all the little suits she'd contrived for him to wear in the midst of their dire poverty, and the love with which she'd filled the humble home.

26

A large delegation had come to the airport to see them off. Elena's parents turned their heads often to wipe away the tears. His two brothers were there, and the union president, the union treasurer, and many near and dear friends. At first the time dragged a bit—as time does in an airport—then suddenly the time is gone, and the loudspeaker utters its imperious command: "Flight ——— is now boarding. All passengers must now board."

He remembered that he had turned back to embrace his father one last time. It had swept over him again that his father and mother had suffered so much from a system of government which might become the government of his new country. Guerrilla warfare had already been going on for several years. Must his father suffer yet again, vicariously? He felt the frail shoulders quiver under his strong young arms, but not one word of regret did Father Silva utter.

For Maria and Lucila, the flight on the plane was the most exciting experience of their young lives. Although eager to see everything they could, they were obedient as always, Maria beside her father and Lucila beside Elena. He had asked for a window seat, and while the plane sat on the runway, and later as it taxied, he tried to take a few pictures of all his loved ones who were standing on the observation deck waving.

Then came a moment that even now, in the despair of his filthy prison, filled his heart with such remembered glory that he caught his breath. As the plane had lifted off the ground into the sunrise, a feeling of total and perfect peace had filled his heart. Gone was every doubt, every misgiving. The presence of God had seemed so real at that moment that he felt almost as though he could touch the hem of His garment. Few moments in life had reached such heights of spiritual exaltation as this one.

After a plane change in Rio de Janeiro, Elena said to her daughters, "Girls, Daddy and I would like to sit together for awhile and talk. The two of you can pretend you're grown-ups and sit in the seats just in front of us."

Charmed by this idea, the two small heads were soon bent over their books and games, though occasional yawns punctuated their concentration.

Antonio and Elena settled in their seats, their hands entwined. Remembering the closeness and sweetness of those hours, Antonio wondered if he were still on the same planet—this planet where reality now was a prison floor with no place to stretch and no apparent hope for the future. But on the flight the two of them had talked of how they'd met and how they'd fallen in love.

"When I began to get acquainted with you, Elena," Antonio had told her, "it seemed to me right from the beginning that the Lord had arranged for us to meet. He meant us for each other."

It was the same old sweet story they'd talked of so many times, but it was always new and wonderful to them.

Elena had squeezed his hand and replied, "Well, I certainly felt that way too, and before I was sure that you did, I was really hoping!"

Leaning his head back against his seat, Antonio had relived those magical days of early love. "Since I was older than most of the other students, it was certainly logical for me to want to marry. But I was wondering how in the world I could support a wife."

Smiling, Elena had interrupted. "But the Lord showed you the way, because when you prayed and said that if it was His will for us to marry, He would enable you to earn the money, just look at what happened!"

Antonio remembered it now, so clearly. He'd read everything he could find in Ellen White's writings regarding Christian marriage, and since he felt totally clear in his choice of a life companion, there remained only that one big word—MONEY.

Then, almost out of nowhere, the conference publishing secretary had asked him if he'd be interested in canvassing at a big military base not too far from the college.

"I must tell you," he had said, "that no colporteur has ever worked there, and I'm not sure you can get permission; but if you can—why, the sky's the limit in what you can sell, I think."

Antonio had been absolutely certain that his prayer was being answered. Teaming up with another theology student, they went through the necessary channels to secure permission for the canvassing. To the surprise of many, it was granted at once, and within three days they had sold so many books that they had earned the equivalent of seven years of full college tuition! Moreover, they soon had secured permission to canvass in yet another army base and DOUBLED the amount of books sold at the first base.

"Well, at least you didn't have to work for me as long as Jacob had to work for Rachel," Elena had chuckled.

"You were already way ahead of me in school," Antonio had reminded Elena. "You had started at the proper time and hadn't had to drop out."

"Yes, I had finished my training as a primary school teacher plus two years of nursing school," Elena reminisced.

Almost in unison, they'd said, "And then we were married, on February 23, 1960."

After sitting silently for a moment, Antonio gently patted Elena's cheek and said, "I thought I was the happiest man in the world that day—but a year later, when Maria came, my heart almost burst with joy."

Again, quiet reflection as the plane droned on, the noise and vibration of the motors making the little girls drowsy. So many fleeting thoughts had come and gone in Antonio's mind—graduation as class president at the college in São Paulo—starting out in his ministerial work with an experienced minister in São Paulo—helping to hold a major effort with over 1200 people in attendance every night—his first very own pastoral district, where Lucila had been born—then pastoring the church at the publishing house in São Paulo—then pastoring the very large college church, the college from which he'd graduated only a few years before—then being chosen president of the Santa Catarina Mission—and now—now he was flying to Africa, flying into the unknown.

Lying on the cold floor of the prison cell, Pastor Silva had been able to lose himself in these thoughts so completely that it was with renewed anguish that he again became aware of his surroundings. The screams and groans and sighs of his cellmates intruded on his reverie. Suddenly his memories became painful. In his president's address at his graduation he had said: "It may be that some one of us will fall in the battlefield against the power of evil. If so, let the inscription in the cemetery say, 'Here lies a man of God.' "

Will I be the first and perhaps the only one in my class to die for my faith? he asked himself. Had he made a prophetic statement in his graduation address? The words ricocheted through his thoughts over and over again.

Then, unbidden, a conversation he'd had a few years before with a fellow minister came into his mind.

"You know, Antonio, I always think of you as one of the very lucky ministers," his friend had said. "You were a delegate to the General Conference session in Atlantic City in North America in 1970. Twice you've been sent to the Andrews University extension courses here in Brazil. Everyone thinks of you as one of the most outstanding speakers we have. Yes, you're lucky."

Antonio had agreed with his friend wholeheartedly that day that his blessings were more than he deserved.

But now—lucky? In this wretched prison?

Pastor Silva instantly put that thought from his mind. He would not, he resolved adamantly, yield to the devil's temptations to self-pity. If he could only sleep, just for a few hours, and forget his unbearable condition! But try as he might and concentrate as he would, sleep would not come. His only consolation was to continue his review of the happy past.

When the big jet had landed in Johannesburg, South Africa, there'd been a weekend of sightseeing with all the charm of a new continent to explore. He and Elena and the little girls had enjoyed the hospitality of the Adventist workers, and had been so grateful to realize, all over again, that "the Adventist family" knows no barriers of race, nationality, or color. But they were eager to get to their "own" country, the one which would become their adopted home for as many years as God might leave them there.

Monday, May 22, 1972, changed their lives forever.

As the small plane began to descend over the capital city in which the mission headquarters was located, Pastor and Mrs. Silva and the little girls peered out with both anticipation and apprehension. In the distance they could see small hutlike structures (later they would learn that these outlying areas were referred to as "the bush") and then the city itself—obviously a contrast between the old and the new, between stark poverty and old customs on the one hand and the adoption of late twentieth century customs on the other.

On that morning, remembered Pastor Silva, I didn't know that this very intermingling of customs was one of the factors seized on by those who were determined to overthrow the existing government. I couldn't know that a particular group would convince the people that all Western influence had enslaved and degraded them, that all people with white skins were bitter enemies to be destroyed.

No such foreshadowing of the future clouded the landing of the plane. The Silvas, however, had their first encounter with entry into a small, underdeveloped country. All the passport inspections, the health card inspections, the customs inspections, and the general "red tape" seemed to go on for hours. But at last the four of them emerged into the lobby of the airport terminal, ready and eager to smile warmly at the people who would be meeting them.

But there was no one to smile at.

They looked this way and that. After all, there hadn't been too many "foreigners" on that plane. Everyone else had been met and accounted for, while they stood alone, a bit forlornly.

"You sent the telegram about our arrival to the mission on Friday when we arrived in Johannesburg, didn't you?" Elena inquired.

"Yes—but something must have gone wrong," Antonio answered.

There on the prison floor, a faint smile crossed his tense face. He was glad that in the beginning of it all, he'd had no idea just how *much* could go wrong, or how even the least undertaking could turn into a nightmare.

On that arrival morning, he'd searched his book for the address of the mission, gathered up the luggage, shepherded his little family out to the curb, and called a taxi. Even that took time and patience. People were milling around, crowding in front of one another, while vendors were hawking wares of various sorts with loud and insistent shouts. Maria's and Lucila's eyes were as big as saucers.

Impulsively he'd turned to Elena.

"I can't tell you how glad and thankful I am that you don't get upset or afraid easily," he told her fondly. "My life would certainly have been more difficult if you hadn't always been full of optimism, always sure that things will turn out right."

Elena blinked in surprise at this glowing compliment, right there on the sidewalk of the airport. She squeezed his arm and smiled in that special way that let him know how much she loved him and valued his good opinion of her.

As the taxi careened along, the four of them swiveled their heads in all directions, trying to see as much as they could. Then suddenly the taxi drew up with a great squealing of brakes in front of—a church.

"Driver," Pastor Silva asked, "are you sure this is the place?"

The driver insisted that this was the address he'd been given. Rather uncertainly, they got themselves and their luggage out of the car and stood on the sidewalk, trying to get their bearings. Just then a basement door flew open, and out rushed a pleasant-looking couple.

"Why, you must be our new president!" they exclaimed. "We're so sorry! Why, if we had known you were coming today we would certainly have been down at the airport to meet you; we've been so eager for you to arrive—your last letter said you'd send a telegram from Johannesburg after you were sure that the plane connections were going to work out . . ."

During this flurry of greeting they had seized the suitcases and were escorting the Silvas into the basement of the church.

"Well, I did send a telegram on Friday from Johannesburg," Pastor Silva assured them. "This is Monday, so I thought that would be more than enough time for it to reach you."

The two of them shook their heads, and the man said, with raised eyebrows, "Who knows when—or if—the telegram will ever arrive? We're so sorry that you got such a poor welcome."

In their gracious way Pastor and Mrs. Silva assured the couple, who turned out to be the mission treasurer and his wife, that they understood perfectly, and that in any case they didn't expect everyone to drop their work just to meet them.

"This is the mission headquarters," the treasurer told Pastor Silva, as he gestured around the small basement which was divided into rooms. Though it was not exactly what the latter had been expecting, his natural flexibility rose to the surface, and he told himself that God's work was more important than physical arrangements.

After they had inspected the offices and met a few of the workers who were there, the treasurer and his wife insisted on taking the Silvas to their own home. "I suppose the first thing you'll want to do is look for a place to live," they said.

Elena agreed wholeheartedly. "Home" was a very important word, especially for Antonio and her. And the little girls needed the security of a place they could count on. Although Elena didn't have any preconceived ideas as to what kind of a place it might be, or any convictions that their living quarters must have this or that feature, during that first afternoon they couldn't find anything suitable. As they knelt that first night in the new land, by the bed so hospitably provided in the treasurer's home, both prayed earnestly that the Lord would soon lead them to a living place, so that Antonio could get into his work.

"Lord, you led us to Africa; I know you have a place for us to live," Antonio prayed.

And the Lord did. The very next day they found a little house, bought mattresses, and slept that night on the floor. Maria and Lucila thought that was really a great idea.

"This is a lot more fun than sleeping in beds," they told their parents, who smiled and silently wished that all the buying of furniture and the settling in were finished.

Eventually the house was made homelike by Elena, but long before that Pastor Silva was deep into his work.

Progress and Peril

Pastor Silva's thoughts, which had winged him out of the cruel prison cell and back to happier days, were disrupted by the pain in his back. Lying as he was in such a cramped position, he felt that soon he, too, would join the chorus of groans.

Perhaps if I stand up for a little while and lean against the wall, my back will stop aching, he said to himself. He noticed that the two pastors who'd been imprisoned with him had fallen into a light sleep. He eased himself to his feet so as not to disturb them. What a blessed period of relief they were having. If only he could sleep also! As he picked his way through the tightly packed bodies and found a spot against the wall, he remembered the joy and exhilaration of those early months in Africa. All his earlier doubts had been swept away on a tide of enthusiasm. He'd plunged all his energies into learning about his new country. He had so many plans, dreams, and ambitions for the Lord's work that it seemed as though the days were never long enough.

The large capital city was populated mostly by blacks, with some Asiatics and a small number of whites. A kind of primitive, pagan religion was the predominant belief, in addition to Islam, Catholicism, and some Protestantism. The climate of the country had two seasons—wet and dry. There were beautiful areas and ugly areas, but the terrain wasn't the important thing. Among the 17,000 baptized Seventh-day Adventist church members and 22,000 Sabbath School members in the entire country, only about 400 were white. These statistics would later be used by a revolutionary government to prove that the whites sought total domination, though just how this could be interpreted was a puzzle.

33

Pastor Silva remembered a conversation he had had with the workers soon after his arrival, when they had explained some of the problems of the field to him.

"You can hardly believe the number of languages and dialects that are spoken in this small country," they told him. "Of course Portuguese is the official language, but you can travel 50 kilometers in one direction and find a certain national language, then travel 50 kilometers in another direction and find a totally different one. The people living that close, when not using Portuguese, can't understand one another in the least."

As Pastor Silva traveled into the bush, he was impressed with the happiness, friendliness, and enthusiasm of the people. Having almost no comforts, living in mud and straw huts, with no prospect of better times for the future, they could still greet each day cheerfully. Immediately drawn to his new people, he committed himself to helping them. He could not have dreamed at that time that shortly the openness of many of the nationals would turn to hostility, as they were conditioned by revolutionary forces to hate "filthy capitalists."

Though many things were forbidden by the government now in power, the establishing of out-schools was not. The children could be taught to read and write Portuguese. Schools could not be established in the cities, however, for there the educational system was totally in the hands of another religious system, which taught its own religion to *all* students.

But in the out-schools, Pastor Silva remembered, as he pressed against the cold wall, "his" people had learned more than reading and writing. Many had been given a chance to read the Bible. Many were baptized. And wonderfully gratifying as this knowledge and commitment was, it was pitifully inadequate as a base for sound planning for the future. Only one "real" school had been permitted the Adventists. Located in a beautiful setting, it was operated somewhat like a boarding school in Brazil or in the United States. But the school had official permission to teach only the four primary grades and two years of Bible training. This represented the sum total of the training available to the national pastors; yet where education ended, the Holy Spirit seemed to take over, and converts to the truth came in by the hundreds.

Tired now of standing against the wall, Pastor Silva picked his way once again through the restless, squirming bodies to his place beside his three friends on the cell floor. In his absence and in their sleep, they'd stretched out a bit more, so that he wondered for a few moments if he could wedge himself into the fast disappearing space. Cramped and miserable, he finally got himself into a semiprone position.

"Oh, God, please help me sleep," he prayed silently. "I must sleep. I don't know what I will face tomorrow. There may be physical torture, and I don't want to deny You no matter what happens. And please, please be with Elena and Maria and Lucila. I know they are so worried and so afraid. Please help them to sleep in spite of their concern for me."

Yet still he remained wide awake, no matter how tightly he shut his eyes, and no matter how deeply and calmly he forced himself to breathe. His troubled thoughts went on and on, as though he were turning over the pages of the book of his life, one at a time.

He hadn't been in his new country long when he became all too aware that national forces were determined to wrest control of the country from the Western power, whose colony it had been for so long. In the northern part of the country guerrilla warfare was so strong and so constant that it had become impossible to travel there and impossible to establish any sort of contact with the believers.

"The guerrilla troops are trained in communist ideology," he was told by others. "Nothing is ever said about this publicly, but their avowed goal is a communist regime and takeover of the country."

He remembered the small, cold chill that had gone down his spine at those words. Memories of the stories his father had told him about life in Siberia, about the torture and death of family members, about the flight through Europe, about the death of the little sister whom he had never seen—all of it passed before his aching eyes. What if . . .? He pushed the negative thoughts away and told himself that, after all, this was a totally different day and age, that world opinion dictates certain standards of governmental conduct, and anyway, it could be decades before any trouble would erupt in the south of his field, where the mission office was located.

Never was faith more generously rewarded than the faith of Pastor Silva in what God could and would accomplish in this African country. As he thought of those years, he began to understand how "stone walls do not a prison make," for his soul rose happy and free, recounting all the fruitful times.

Elena had plunged into mission life with such verve and enthusiasm that certainly the Adventist Church had secured "two for the price of one.'' She was here, there, and everywhere, holding vacation Bible schools, teaching cooking classes, visiting the sick, traveling with Antonio whenever proper care for Maria and Lucila could be arranged—and she hadn't done all this grudgingly, he recalled, smiling in the half-dark. She'd been happy, vibrant, enthusiastic, as only Elena could be. She'd never once reproached him for taking the family away from their home country. She continued to provide a warm, loving homelife. Because of her strong mothering, Maria and Lucila had adjusted to their new life so quickly and completely that every day he felt grateful.

But did he, even then, have some sort of premonition about the future? I don't know why I worked as though some sort of time limit were being placed on me, he said to himself. I just couldn't rest. I seemed to have the energy of three men. I prepared Bible studies in six native languages. I held seminars with workers all over the country (except in those areas which were guerrilla-dominated) training them to give Bible studies. I called one workers' meeting after another to review carefully all our principal doctrines with my national pastors, so they would be firmly grounded. It seemed very, very important to do this and do it at once.

Then he'd had the feeling that even though others in the country who'd been there longer thought literature evangelism wasn't too successful, he must encourage it. He'd launched a strong campaign to reactivate this phase of the gospel.

His shoulders aching from the stone floor, Pastor Silva thought of the mornings when he couldn't wait to get up and start working. Teachers needed more training, more out-schools must be opened, and—one of his most cherished projects—a countrywide campaign to enroll people in the Bible correspondence course must be announced in all the main newspapers. To augment the newspaper advertisements, pamphlets were printed and distributed all over the country.

We worked so hard that it seems now we were on some kind of a countdown basis, he said to himself. And it paid off. When baptisms reached a thousand a year and kept on climbing, Pastor Silva had told his workers that they should aim at three and four thousand a year. He had not had, he remembered, the slightest doubt that this goal would be reached.

But the clouds on the political horizon were growing ever darker. Almost overnight it seemed, Pastor Silva could not return to areas where he had visited only a few months before. The guerrilla fighters had started hiding bombs in the roads. As the cars drove over them, the explosions took many lives. Or the guerrillas would conceal themselves in the bush and when a vehicle passed, they would attack with machine guns. When the national army tried to locate and deal with them, they simply dissolved into the great, all-encompassing African bush. Railroad trains were bombed, with great loss of life. The violence never stopped.

Pastor Silva remembered that Elena had tried hard not to show her fear for him on his travels. He remembered one morning when he was starting out for a "marginal" area where guerrillas were reported to be active.

"You will be careful, won't you, love?" she had asked him wistfully, her dark eyes soft and concerned.

"You know I will, my darling," he had replied, putting his arm about her lovingly.

"I'm not asking you not to go," she murmured, her head against his shoulder. "I know you are doing God's work, but I'll be praying every minute."

As the situation became more tense, the two of them seldom spoke of the dangers on every hand. Danger was something with which they must live. But the sun didn't seem quite as bright now, and the little house, with its plain furnishings, seemed dearer to him every time he returned from a bush trip.

Though he could not know it then, Pastor Silva's destiny was being decided thousands of miles across the sea, in the Western country which controlled the small African country. A military revolution took place in that Western country, offering all sorts of promises regarding the future of their homeland and colonies. One of those promises stated that the African country could hold a plebiscite to determine whether it wanted to be independent, even though economically and socially it was tragically unready. This was what the well-organized guerrillas had been waiting for. Their orders and plans were laid out for them in yet another country skilled in violent revolution. The plans were executed to the letter by nationals from the "planning" country, who had "innocently" infiltrated.

In a show of frightening power, the guerrillas had sealed off all the roads in the country, mined them, and proclaimed themselves the official government of the nation. The Western power, much weakened by internal strife, could not spare the manpower to send in troops, and so on a fateful September day a treaty was signed. The national plebiscite was bypassed. The proviso of the treaty was that a transitional government would be formed; in one year this government would have full and complete power.

Pastor Silva shuddered there on the cell floor, realizing that from that September day, terror had begun.

Many elements eventually conspired to bring a chaos that led to iron repression. First of all, other political groups in the country objected violently to the power which had been seized by the guerrillas. They saw their slender hold on any semblance of power slipping from their grasp. Most frightening of all, from the viewpoint of the expatriate Adventist workers at the mission headquarters, was the technique immediately employed by the guerrilla leaders—the deliberate inflaming of racial hatred via the newspapers, radio, billboards, placards, and word of mouth. Blacks were bombarded ceaselessly with propaganda stating that all their troubles, all their deprivation, all their lack of progress, could be traced directly to the Western whites who had controlled the country.

Pastor Silva had found himself sympathetic with the fact that injustices had been done. Fair play had not always been the rule. Not for a moment did he deny any of the real truth, but he knew that much of what was said was greatly exaggerated. It was so inflammatory that it could lead to only one thing—more violence.

And so the national terror began. Wave after wave of violence swept over the small country, leaving death and fear in its wake. Almost overnight the entire atmosphere changed. Pastor Silva remembered the first few nights when he and Elena and the little girls had gone to bed, only to be awakened by the sound of gunfire in the streets. He remembered how Elena had run to the little girls' bedroom to make them feel safe.

"Don't worry, dears," she had told them, comforting them in her arms. "We are safe here in our house, and God will take care of us."

They had gone back to sleep, trusting their mother and father as they had always done. But he and Elena had lain silently side by side, each with thoughts too ominous to be shared. Finally they grew accustomed to the night violence, if one ever does get used to such things.

Lying there on the cell floor, Pastor Silva's eyes opened wide and stared into the dim room, as he lived again the period of time when hatred for "Europeans" had escalated. Children on their way home from school would be set upon in the streets. On several occasions, members of a gang would hold a child down on the ground while another member with the back of an ax, would smash the small head to pieces. White farmers—and their white cattle—and white chickens—were put to death; some were tortured and disemboweled, and the animals suffered agonizingly slow deaths. Madness seemed loose in the land.

When a number of cars containing Europeans had been stoned, fire bombs thrown into them, and the motorists incinerated, Pastor Silva had begun to have very serious thoughts about Elena and Maria and Lucila. As yet he hadn't come to the point of wondering if the three should return to Brazil. The family closeness seemed to blank out even a hint of that solution. But he now began to think very carefully of such an eventuality.

One day he had asked the three of them to sit down and have a talk with him.

"We all know that street fighting is everywhere. We just have to live with it," he explained, not wishing to alarm the little girls unduly. He didn't need to worry about Elena; he almost smiled to himself, wondering just how much it would have taken to frighten her indomitable spirit. Going on, though, he suggested, "If you're ever caught out on the streets and fighting begins, remember that the first thing to do is drop to the ground and lie as flat and still as you can. Guns are fired at targets that move."

Solemnly, Maria and Lucila promised him that at the first hint of such an experience, they'd follow his directions to the letter.

He couldn't know then how important this talk would be. But only a few days later, when Elena took Lucila along to the large open-air market where they had to purchase their food each day, shooting broke out. Quick as a wink the little girl hurled herself on the ground—but she didn't stop there. She wormed her way underneath cases of lettuce and tomatoes. She refused to budge until all was quiet.

Elena, in telling him about it later in the day, couldn't restrain her chuckles.

"There was Lucila, looking like a very large salad," she smiled. "I hope the lettuce and tomatoes weren't any the worse for the experience."

He had laughed also and praised Lucila highly. But a cold finger of fear had touched his heart as he clasped the small, precious, warm body in his arms.

Then a wholesale exodus of all Europeans began, including others who were able to convert their holdings into cash and secure air tickets out—provided they had someplace to start a new life. People were frantically trying to sell their property and household goods at a reduced rate. But there were few "takers." The future was too uncertain.

Thinking all this over, Elena had said to Antonio, "You know, a few months ago many of these people wouldn't have thought of giving their property to any kind of religious group. They wanted to hang onto everything they possibly could. Now all their possessions are almost worthless to them."

Her words were prophetic; soon people would beg the Seventh-day Adventist mission to take their property—and it would be too late.

But at this point, in spite of all the unrest and real danger, Pastor Silva remembered that it had been a brief time of great opportunity for the church. Gradually the civil unrest was brought under some kind of control. For the first time, and to his astonishment, he secured permission for a large public evangelistic effort to be held downtown in the capital city. Moreover, the transitional government in power allowed the churches to register their property and announced that there would be no religious restrictions.

This "reprieve" was short-lived. Pastor Silva and his workers soon discovered that the registration of all church properties and organizations had been part of a careful plan. Beginning with each block of houses in the city, and in every industry, every school, every hospital, and every bush village—leaders were appointed to hold weekly political discussions.

"This is the very flowering of democracy," the people were told. "This is how you will learn to live democratically, since you have thrown off the iron heel of the Western oppressors."

A carefully orchestrated roster of subjects was discussed—independence, liberty, freedom, social behavior, political education, objectives of the new party, and so on. Who would *dare* to criticize such a lofty plan to bring long-mistreated nationals into the late twentieth century?

Smoothly, the designated officials had approached Pastor Silva.

"We will be holding weekly meetings in your main school and in your bush schools—with your permission, of course," they informed him.

Gazing across his desk at the expressionless faces of the men, he knew that a charade was being played out. His permission meant nothing. The meetings would be held regardless. His refusal could only cause trouble for the national believers. But would the scriptural foundation the young people had been learning be sufficient to counteract the spurious teachings that would be drummed into their ears? Would all the years of effort be wasted? Would young Christians become spiritual casualties, crushed by a system opposed to God? These were questions he could not answer. He could only pray silently.

Then, with impeccable manners, Pastor Silva had replied, "We shall accept you as guests in our schools."

As the men in the cell around him groaned and twisted and turned, he clearly remembered how, though the meetings were announced as learning sessions in furthering the great cause of democracy, they soon turned into persistent questioning sessions in which the students were grilled regarding the expatriate missionaries and their own national church leaders.

"Do you have any complaints?" they were asked again and again. "Are your church leaders loyal to our government?" Because students are students the world over, some in any group are bound to feel hostile to teachers who are charged with responsibility for proper behavior and learning. When unwise comments were forced from them, a careful record was made for future use.

Restlessly Pastor Silva reviewed the inexorable march of events: the growing political power of the "thought groups" and later, their direct accountability only to the President; the crumbling of the public administration of the country; the handing over of complex departments to nationals who had had no training, no schooling, no background in administration; the stark fact that only political militants received administrative positions, no matter how unqualified they were; the frantic confusion everywhere; the total disruption of life for the people.

Yet every day, all day and most of the night, by radio, newspaper, and public meetings, the people were actually being hypnotized with such ringing phrases as, "Justice for all at last!" "This country for its own people!" "Riches for the people!" "Freedom for the people!" And in the shops supplies dwindled, so that the daily foray for food was a major undertaking. Elena didn't complain, though. As the situation worsened, she had seemed to grow stronger, her eyes brighter, her step firmer, her resolve to cope more decided.

Not all the missionaries had shared his and Elena's attitude, though, and some had felt that they must return to their homelands. For this he had not blamed them. No one can fully enter into the pressures and fears in the hearts of others. For himself, he only knew that he seemed to be working under some kind of premonition. But then he shook off his forebodings. He'd always been a hard worker. This was nothing new. And yet he knew there was something different about it. His overriding compulsion during this period was to train his national workers as thoroughly as possible. They must know more and more and more. He held seminars endlessly and drilled the national pastors in doctrines and soul winning.

Then the year of the provisional government ended—time for the "official" government to take office. Would he ever forget that night? he wondered to himself. Hundreds of thousands of people milled about in the city and throughout the countryside. The speeches went on all night, as did the feasting, the dancing, and the drinking. He had advised his workers that it would probably be best for them to listen to the festivities on the radio in the safety of their homes, which they did. Another Protestant group—one of whose main tenets is nonallegiance to temporal governments—seized the night of the independence to stage a massive distribution of their literature to nearly every house in the city. Perhaps they felt that this would be their last opportunity. Their unwise move was to bear bitter fruit later in the suspicion and persecution directed at all Protestant groups.

Searching his soul in that wretched cell, Pastor Silva could find no fault with the way he had led his people through this treacherous time. Using the text, "Render therefore unto Caesar the things which are Caesar's" and taking the position that until the new government had asked of them what they could not give, he counseled his co-workers and all the Adventist believers to maintain a stance of loyalty. They did not criticize. They did not attempt to tear down.

Then came the "great" day that the people had been told to wait for. The new constitution was announced. Unbelievingly, Pastor Silva and his workers read that one of the articles granted religious freedom! Moreover, the constitution subscribed to the United Nations Human Rights charter. Had God worked a very special miracle just for his people in this African country so far from the mainstream of modern life?

Sadly now, Pastor Silva recalled that the relief experienced by the believers had been so great that prayer and praise services of thanksgiving had been held in some of the churches.

Through all the political unrest of the transitional government, Pastor Silva and his staff had been searching for a new office building to replace the pitifully inadequate church basement. It had seemed as though their search would never end successfully—and yet it had. Some time before independence they moved into it. They had managed to secure funds to buy a much nicer building than first they'd hoped for—a three-story building on a handsome main street near the best hospital of the city. On the first floor they made alterations to accommodate the receptionist, cashier, treasury, Book and Bible House, and two departmental offices. They had put the Bible Correspondence School, a worship and committee room, and various other offices on the second floor.

Now Pastor Silva's thoughts became so painful that he could feel the tears welling up in his eyes; the third floor had become an apartment for Elena and the little girls and himself.

"Dearest," he had told Elena when it was settled, "what a relief it's going to be for me to know that you and Maria and Lucila are upstairs. I won't be worried about all those blocks between the office and our home and what could happen to you walking back and forth when I'm not here. Maria and Lucila can play in the yard where we can have them in sight at all times. Besides, there's a good high fence and shrubbery for protection."

Elena hugged him. "I've never been really afraid when you're out of town, though once in awhile I've been just a *tiny* bit worried. But living here in this office building; I don't think I'll be one bit nervous!" she assured him.

A tear rolled slowly down his cheek as he remembered that dearly loved apartment. He could not know when he moved in that he would live there for only a few months and that from there he would go to prison, never to see his home and his simple but cherished possessions again.

But a welcome respite had developed, though the Silvas had been almost too busy to think about it. Pastor Silva had been selected as a delegate to attend the General Conference session in Vienna, Austria! Elena's face had lighted up like a young girl's when he told her.

"Why, Antonio! Whoever thought that you and I would see *Europe?* God is just too good to us! We're too lucky!" she had cried, and in his heart he had echoed her feelings.

"Yes," he told her fondly, "we're lucky, but I'm the most fortunate, for I have you as my wife.''

Actually, the Silvas should have returned to Brazil for their first furlough before this time, but with such unrest and with Pastor Silva's compulsion to accomplish all that he could in the shortest time, he had kept postponing the furlough. Elena, though wistful, had not tried to change his mind. Then when the Vienna trip materialized, he was glad he had postponed his furlough, for now they could go to Europe, then to Brazil, and then back to Africa.

He now remembered how he had worried through those busy years, about his parents—aging, ever aging—how faithfully he'd written to them, and how faithfully they had written back with never a word of discouragement. Elena's parents had been equally supportive. Of course he and Elena had been united in their resolve to paint as favorable a picture of conditions in Africa as possible, though they hadn't always been successful. Newspaper accounts filtering out of their turbulent country had often disquieted the older people, but they'd taken their fears to God—to whom they had always taken them throughout their lifetime.

''The Lord has been so good,'' Antonio told Elena as they packed for Vienna. ''Our parents' lives have been preserved. Now we're going to see them again and have a wonderful visit, but on top of that, we're going to see Europe.''

That's how it turned out. Never did four people more enjoy a new continent and a General Conference session and a glorious reunion with loved ones. What a bright and beautiful world it was!

Pastor Silva could not know that this happy world would soon be destroyed. Lying there on the cold stone floor, he thought of the first strong indications that a tremendous storm was about to break in his African country. While on furlough his treasurer wrote him several times, telling him about the violent changes and of his fears and uncertainties for the future.

Drastic changes had been taking place almost overnight while Pastor Silva was on furlough. First there was the loss of the two medical dispensaries. One was especially new and well-equipped. In one day it was decreed that all medical and educational institutions were now ''nationalized.'' On the following morning soldiers with machine guns stood in front of it; sadly, the dedicated Adventist personnel observed from a distance and did not even go near, fearing for their lives. After some days had passed, the government reopened the dispensary with non-Adventist personnel, each staff member

44

being a "tried and true" militant. No explanation was ever given for the takeover, no financial compensation ever received by the mission.

When the letter describing the takeover arrived in Brazil, Pastor Silva read it aloud to Elena. "I just can't believe it!" she gasped. "Our lovely dispensary which was doing such a good work. We must pray that the Lord will work on the hearts of the present government officials to restore it to us."

But more trouble was to come. The next letter brought news that the boarding school was now in the possession of the state, but in this case a few Adventists had been part of the "committee" and so Pastor Silva felt that the institution might still in some small way continue to quietly spread the gospel.

One morning upon receipt of yet another letter, Pastor Silva opened it quickly, scanned it rapidly, then blurted out, "Elena, listen to this! A group of men entered the mission office, announced that they were from the government, ordered the cashier to hand over all the money in the safe, and then took it away with them. On the day when the checks were to be sent to the north part of the country to pay the salary of eighty of our workers, the bank notified our treasurer that our bank account could no longer be used. Oh, the poor, poor people! How can they exist with no money!"

In the peaceful bedroom of Elena's parents' home in Brazil, the two of them knelt and implored God to provide—somehow, some way—for the national workers. They had tried to put all the disquieting news out of their minds and treasure each moment with the two sets of parents, the brothers and their families, and the loving friends. Maria and Lucila, with the innocence and unawareness of childhood, were as active and happy as two butterflies, though Maria was now on the verge of young womanhood and understood much more of the true situation than Pastor Silva would have liked.

When yet another letter arrived, there was nothing on the outside of the envelope to indicate that this piece of folded paper would seal the fate of Pastor Silva. On the floor of the prison cell, Antonio thought that it should have been bordered in black.

"A government order has been issued stating that all foreigners now outside this country will lose their visas unless they return in not more than ninety days," his treasurer had written. "I know that because of your attendance at the session in Vienna you would normally be staying in Brazil a little longer; but I thought that I must tell you that, unless you return at once, you will never be able to reenter.''

"Antonio!'' Elena exclaimed in alarm. "Your face has gone white as a sheet. What is in the letter?''

Silently he had handed it to her. After she read it, she put her hand in his, but said nothing. Before they had left for Vienna, the mission treasurer had been deeply agitated. "You will never return. I am sure,'' he had told them. "I wouldn't blame you, for things in this country are so terrible. But if you don't come back, all the other expatriate missionaries will leave also, and then what will happen to God's work?''

Pastor Silva had placed his hand firmly on the treasurer's arm. "I *will* return—that I promise you,'' he told him quietly. "If you will carry on as best you can during the three months I am away, you can count on my return if the Lord allows me to live. I must, though, go home and see my dear, aged parents.''

"Oh, I know that, and I'm sorry to sound selfish. I wouldn't stand in your way—but we need you desperately here.''

Sitting in the quiet room in Brazil, Pastor Silva remembered that conversation. But his duty was now very clear to him. He must go back in order to stay within the ninety-day limit. "If after we have been there a short time it becomes clear that the expatriates must leave, then we will always know that we did all we could and that we did not let the Lord down,'' he told Elena, knowing that he could count on her quick agreement.

During these long night hours on the floor of the prison cell, Pastor Silva had found some of his memories almost too painful to recall. He nearly groaned aloud as he remembered the scene that took place when he told his mother and his father that he must return at once to Africa.

His mother, always so perfectly controlled, burst into sobs.

"My dear, dear son, please, I beg of you, do not go back,'' she wept. "I know what can happen in governments like these. People lose all their rights; they lose all legal protection. You have done your work out there in that troubled land. The Lord will not hold you accountable for not returning. And besides, think of your duty to Elena and Maria and Lucila.''

He could not hold back the tears himself as he saw and felt her sorrow and fear.

"Mother dear,'' he had told her, holding her frail hands in his,

46

"God is telling me that I must go. But He will protect me, and He will protect Elena and the girls. But I make you this promise. After we have been there briefly and have investigated the situation carefully, if I find that it is hopeless, we shall return and be with you here in Brazil for many years."

Her continued quiet sobbing, her silent despair, had been like hammer blows to his heart. Thinking of it now, his faith almost wavered for a moment. Had God been speaking through his mother? Should he have listened and remained in Brazil?

Ominous Developments

When the plane landed at the now-familiar airport, the Silvas were prepared for the "red tape" which they had encountered on their first entry—but they were not prepared for the hostility and suspicion with which the various officials treated them. After they had disembarked and entered the airport, they went by a desk where a uniformed man demanded harshly, "How much foreign money do you have in your possession?"

After the two of them had counted their money (the girls were not carrying any) they were handed a slip of paper and told to write the exact total. Next, with thinly-veiled insolence, their passports were minutely examined, and eventually the required entry permit was stamped on them. Then, presentation of their World Health Cards, with another minute inspection of their inoculation records. After that, customs, with the contents of their suitcases being examined inch by inch.

At this point they thought they were through and would be admitted into the main lobby. But no. As they passed another uniformed man, who was conspicuously wearing a gun, he demanded coldly, "Empty your pockets and put all your money on the desk."

Their hearts beating hard, though they had nothing to hide, Pastor and Mrs. Silva had complied with the order. The official counted their money several times, then made a careful notation on the slip which they had signed earlier and which (as if by magic) had appeared on his desk.

"I'm afraid to think what would happen if someone had made an innocent mistake in counting and the totals weren't the same," Elena whispered to Antonio.

"It's obvious that some pitfalls have been arranged for foreigners," he whispered back.

But now they were going through the large doors which separated the incoming passengers from those waiting to greet them. There, waiting to receive them with wide, happy smiles, were the mission treasurer and a large group of Adventist believers from the churches in the city. The treasurer literally ran through the milling crowd and threw his arms around Pastor Silva.

"I just can't believe you're here!" he exclaimed. "I just can't believe it! Now things will be all right. I won't have to make all these hard decisions by myself." Pastor Silva could see that his co-worker was in the grip of very deep emotion. He pondered, briefly, what it meant, but then it was all hurry and bustle, greeting the members and getting into the car to start the trip across the city.

Maria and Lucila burst out, "Something's different—why, now I see what it is—all the lovely monuments have been torn down!"

Unbelievingly the four of them gazed at the public squares which, when they had left only three months before, had harbored monuments—many of them real works of art—commemorating various heroes of the Western power which had colonized and protected this small country. They were all gone, smashed to rubble, with the pieces lying on the ground for all to see.

Pastor Silva suddenly remembered, there in the prison cell, that as he'd gazed at the smashed monuments, he'd heard the echo of his mother's voice as she had pleaded with him: "Don't go back, Son; please don't go back. You don't know what can happen in such political situations."

But he had resolutely pushed these thoughts aside, and he and Elena and the girls expressed their joy as the car had drawn up in front of the mission office.

Flinging open the door of their third-floor apartment, Pastor Silva had expressed the feeling of all of them, "It's good to be home again!"

Elena had smiled at him. She knew how much home meant to him.

Almost immediately though, he'd been plunged into problems that were insoluble: first, "nationalization of property," which meant that any property not being lived on by those who owned it could be claimed by someone else, with no monetary compensation being given to the rightful owner.

"We must get some of our believers with large families to move to every piece of land we own; into every church building and every day

49

school,'' Pastor Silva told his staff. What an undertaking that had been! It meant hours and days and weeks of contacting believers, of finding people who could leave their own places with a family member in residence, so that their own small properties were protected.

One night, near midnight, while Pastor Silva was still working in his office, trying to create some semblance of order out of hopeless confusion, Elena tiptoed down the stairs and stood behind him, her hands on his shoulders.

"Don't you think that you had better come to bed now, dear?" she had asked. "You'll be rested in the morning, and it will be easier."

He'd allowed himself to be persuaded, for he was bone-tired. But at the back of his mind was that nagging sense of urgency. "Work, for the night is coming"—the words of the old hymn kept running through his mind.

Actually, he told himself, tossing and turning on the prison floor, it was strange that so much was different at that time, but that other matters proceeded in a fairly normal way. Part of the world church's Thirteenth Sabbath Offering for that quarter was to be applied to the building of an academy on the land where the medical dispensary had been nationalized! He'd taken a trip to visit the site and had found things going well. Encouraged, he'd returned to the capital city, only to find problems of yet a different kind.

Another government decree announced that all religious groups would be supported officially by the government. No churches would be managed from outside the country. "Our country for us" was the general tenor of the new philosophy, with total disregard for the money from overseas which had largely established the religious work that had proved of such great benefit to the people.

From another direction came problems of a different sort. It was too much to expect that all Adventist members were completely loyal to the church; it would be too much to expect in any country. There are always those in any religious organization who choose to relax their commitment to the principles of their church yet who become enraged when, after being prayed with and counseled, they are finally and reluctantly disfellowshiped.

Just such a group of disgruntled, disfellowshiped former Adventists had demanded a hearing with Pastor Silva at the mission office. About twenty men crowded into the building, obviously determined to have things their way.

At first the conversation was fairly quiet and amicable. They stated their demands. They insisted that they be reinstated as members in good and regular standing of the Adventist Church.

Pastor Silva listened courteously.

"But to be an Adventist in good and regular standing, you must believe in certain biblical principles, and your actions must demonstrate your belief," he told them. "This is what the *Church Manual* says."

Raising their voices to a threatening shout, the men crowded close.

"That *Church Manual* is not for our country," they told him. "It was printed in another country, and we don't have to abide by it." (Later Pastor Silva would discover that they had been given this word by the new government.)

Unbelievingly, he had stared at these people whom he knew so well. Had it already come to this? Then the men began to mutter other comments, ask questions under their breath, and make accusations which Pastor Silva could not understand. What was it all about? What did they really want? What was their real purpose?

After the crowd of angry men left the office, his treasurer had said, "Pastor, this same group came here while you were on furlough and said some of the same things to me. Something is going on, something that is frightening. We will know what it is, sooner or later."

Now, lying on the cell floor, Pastor Silva wondered if these people were in league with certain terrorists to destroy the Adventist Church and to bring as much harm as possible to expatriate workers—whose only crime had been to work as hard for the nationals as they could.

Now each day had become so tension-filled that restful sleep at night was hard to achieve. Pastor Silva, after much prayer and consultation with his staff, had decided that they should plan as carefully and minutely for the next three months as possible. No one knew what each day would bring, but as long as he was there, along with other expatriates, he and the others should make their presence count. They all agreed.

On the very day that they worked out itineraries for the projected three months, they discovered that missionaries of other denominations—people they knew as friends—were being taken to prison. Like a rapidly accelerating vehicle, the tempo of terror increased.

—Religion began to be identified via the radio and newspapers as the tool of international imperialism to "tame" the populace so they could be exploited by capitalism.

—Missionaries were declared to be the instruments of this "colonialistic exploitation."

—Films were shown constantly in theatres and museums which ridiculed religion.

—Articles were published giving specific allegations of the "crimes" of missionaries.

At breakfast one morning, as she was looking at the newspaper, Elena gasped: "Antonio, listen to this!" Then she read him a long front-page story about a Nazarene missionary who had been imprisoned. He was said to have sent great quantities of money out of the country to the United States. A whole table of figures was published as "proof" of his "crime."

Pastor Silva listened, sick at heart.

"Elena," he said, "that is absolutely, totally untrue. The letters and records have been falsified. We both know that with the income level as low as it is in this country, no religious group could even exist here without great quantities of money being given from overseas."

He pondered silently for a moment. "For every ten dollars we spend in this country, eight are contributions from Western countries," he declared.

But conditions continued to worsen. Now it took a good deal of Pastor Silva's time to keep constantly informed of each new development, so that he would know what steps should be taken to protect the mission and all denominational property in the country, as well as his workers. Catholic priests were being expelled with much fanfare. Protestant ministers who were fortunate suffered the same fate. Others were sent to prison.

Although Elena had begun to look tired and drawn, with her customary optimism she insisted that they would stay as long as they could be of help. Then they would have to leave for the sake of Maria and Lucila. As for the girls, they had become increasingly aware of the dangers on every hand. They never strayed away from the grounds of the mission office, but stayed very, very close in the yard.

In talking with his treasurer, Pastor Silva outlined a plan.

"I'm going to secure the addresses and working hours of all the foreign consulates and embassies here in the city," he announced. "Our former division president, when he saw what had begun to happen here a few years ago, told me that this would be a vital thing to do. We don't know at what time of the day or night we might need help."

Pastor Silva had many opportunities to thank God for this wise counsel. But he went a step further. He made a careful record of the passport numbers of all the expatriate missionaries and their children. It was his intention to secure visas which would allow all of these people to enter South Africa if an emergency should arise. But when he went to the embassy of South Africa, it had been closed. However, he discovered that a consulate had been established in the city, and he went there for the visas. After listening to his rather unusual request, the official said, "But visas are given for specific trips, for specific periods of time. They are not given in a general way for an undisclosed time."

Pastor Silva replied, "I am aware of that, and I know that my request is irregular, but you have observed conditions here as I have. You know that expatriates might have to leave abruptly. Is there any way you could make an exception and grant the visas?"

The official pondered for a moment. "I will send the request to our capital, Pretoria," he agreed.

While waiting anxiously to see if the visas would be granted, Pastor Silva received word from his division president requesting him to send all the names, passport numbers, and other vital information to the South African Union Conference, so that leaders in that area could work directly with the officials in Pretoria and expedite the visas.

At last the word came. The visas would be granted! Pastor Silva should take all the passports to the consulate to have the visas stamped on them. Just as he was assembling all the documents, a telephone call came. "The consulate has closed its doors. No one knows when it will reopen," the caller informed him. And it didn't reopen. Time elapsed, so that even this protection was not forthcoming.

Lying there on the floor of the prison cell, he asked himself, Did I do everything that I possibly could to protect my people? Did I do my best? Even in the anguish of the moment, though, he could not think of anything that he had left undone.

During this period he and Elena felt much like people who see a huge and ugly storm approaching, who fear what it may do but are not sure just how and where it will strike. He remembered, for instance, a political rally which had been held in a huge soccer stadium. Many thousands cheered the government spokesman. The latter eulogized the people who had "overthrown imperialism" and thrown off the "chains of injustice." As he screamed louder and louder, the people became almost hysterical.

Suddenly, like lightning, when he had them completely in his power, he thundered, "But there is a group of people in this country who do not come to our rallies and our patriotic dances. They do not salute our flag. They are the Jehovah's Witnesses!"

The crowd roared with rage.

"What shall we do with these troublemakers, these enemies of our country?" he demanded.

From the thousands of throats thundered back the response, "Reeducate them! Reeducate them!" And the chant continued over and over, mindlessly.

Antonio and Elena, listening to their radio in their little apartment, had felt their blood turn to ice. "It sounds like the description in the Bible of Jesus before Pilate, when the mob shouted, "Crucify Him! Crucify Him!" Elena whispered.

On succeeding days after the frightening "patriotic rally," trucks stopped in front of the homes of the Jehovah's Witnesses and took all the families to prison—the men, the women, and the children. They were given no chance to defend themselves. They simply dropped out of sight. Driving by the prison one night, Pastor Silva and Elena encountered a large crowd of people standing about, some weeping, others praying. They stopped to see if they could help.

"We are Jehovah's Witnesses—our relatives have been put into this prison—we can't find out anything about them—we don't know if they're dead or alive," a tearful elderly woman told them.

Pastor Silva's thoughts, there in the prison cell, were too deep for tears. I could not know, he thought, that in just a few days after that evening I would be in that same prison—that I would be where I am tonight.

But in counsel with his workers, Pastor Silva had stressed the fact that the Adventist Church stays strictly out of politics, that it is careful to obey the laws and to cooperate without compromise. There was still so much to be done, so many people to be helped. Careful as they all were, surely there would be no danger.

Then the head of the publishing work, a friend whom he had called from Brazil to assume this work, asked to talk with him.

"I have some very uneasy feelings about our colporteurs continuing to go from door to door selling our books," he told Pastor Silva. "Suppose they should be seized. How could we help them?"

Pastor Silva thought for a moment. Then he spoke slowly. "Well—the publishing work has actually been newly legalized by the government, from what we read in the papers. No prohibition on door-to-door selling of religious literature has been announced."

Both the men sat silently for a moment, weighing all angles of the situation. Then Pastor Silva said, "Let's go on with selling our literature as long as we can. But let's tell our colporteurs not to ask people to enroll in the Bible Correspondence School. That might be construed as subversive."

Pastor Silva remembered that the new government had actually prohibited almost nothing. Religious freedom had continued to be widely advertised in all the media. But thinking it over now in the cell, he remembered bitterly that only when something had been done in innocence was the person arrested and imprisoned. It had been like flying an aircraft with no radar and landing at a completely dark airport in the middle of the night. But they had prayed earnestly that God would help them steer their way carefully.

Now events had begun to move forward with accelerating speed. On Wednesday, October 22, a worker burst into the mission office with the news that one of the young colporteurs had been seized and imprisoned. Aghast, Pastor Silva called his staff together.

"We talked all this out very carefully before advising the colporteurs to continue," he told them. "The selling of religous literature has been relegalized—we made sure of that."

"Then possibly that isn't the reason he was jailed," one of the other workers suggested.

"What else could it possibly be, though?" another asked.

Deciding that conversation and speculation were useless at that point, Pastor Silva felt the important thing was to find out exactly what had happened and why. If there were a secret law forbidding the sale of religious literature, they must find this out without a moment's delay, and get the word to all the colporteurs throughout the country.

After evening prayers, Pastor Silva came to some conclusions. "I think," he told his Brazilian publishing secretary, "that you had better cancel your itinerary, and you and I will spend all our time on this matter until we get it cleared up—or at least until we find out all we can."

Most of Thursday was spent notifying the various areas that the publishing secretary would not be coming. Pastor Silva attended to as much of the stacked-up business on his desk as he could, working feverishly. But there was still so much that needed doing—so many items that only he could take care of.

His publishing secretary realized how harassed he was.

"Early tomorrow morning I'll take the local mission president with me, and we'll start out, looking for our worker," he told Pastor Silva. "I think we can manage without you; but we'll report back from time to time, and if we need your help, then you'll be available.

Thankfully, Pastor Silva agreed to the plan, for he hadn't been able to really catch up on his work since returning from furlough.

He could not know that Friday would change his life.

"Imprison Him!"

It began as a day like all others in that lovely country. The weather was perfect, with brilliant sunshine; the tropical flowers bloomed in their usual profusion. Of course it was special, as all Fridays are, for it was the preparation day for the Sabbath.

As was their custom, Pastor and Mrs. Silva and Maria and Lucila gathered in their pleasant living room in the third-floor apartment, read the Morning Watch message for the day, studied the Sabbath School lesson, and talked a few moments before they had their prayer.

"You know," Elena said, "if a few years ago someone had told us that we would become used to the way we now live, I suppose we wouldn't have believed it. Every day would have seemed like a catastrophe, but we're so used to arrests, food shortages, people trying to leave the country, the struggle to get airline tickets, the violence, and all the rest that we just accept it as a natural thing."

"Well, maybe not entirely natural, but I want to tell the three of you how proud I am of your courage and cheerfulness," Pastor Silva said, smiling at them. "You really are my sunshine, no matter what happens outside our home."

Then they knelt, and as he thought of it now in the prison cell, he wondered. Had their prayers for divine protection and guidance been just a little more fervent than usual? Had they pleaded with God for more of His special watchcare than at other times? He would never know, for they had uttered so many prayers of this sort in the harrowing months that they had lived through.

Breakfast in the sunny dining room was cheery and delightful as always. Then Pastor Silva went downstairs to his office to conduct the workers' morning worship period. Days begin early in the tropics, and usually a rest period takes place in the heat of the day, though on Friday they would close the office at noon. Attending worship that morning were the treasurer and his wife, the latter also acting as accountant and secretary. Pastor Silva's secretary was present; in addition to her secretarial duties, she was in charge of the Bible Correspondence School.

Not seeing the publishing secretary, Pastor Silva assumed that he had already started his investigation regarding the imprisoned colporteur. The publishing secretary's son, who was at that time taking care of the Book and Bible Office, attended as did two office boys who were helping out. Joining the group were a president and treasurer of a local mission, the two of them being temporarily quartered in the office building.

Knowing that the publishing secretary and a local mission president were on their special assignment, the worshipers that morning were very serious. Though there had been scares before and many threats had been made to workers and to laity, though property had been confiscated and violence had been done, this was the first time that a worker had been imprisoned. Was it the beginning of the end for God's work in this lovely country?

Although Pastor Silva worked at his desk after worship, he felt a great need to get out of the office and do his own investigating.

To his secretary he said, "It suddenly occurs to me that there's a man downtown who's always well-informed about everything that's going on in the religious community. You know who I mean—the manager of the non-denominational Bible Society. I'll just hop into my car and go down to his office and see what I can find out. I won't be gone more than half an hour."

Suiting the action to the word, he'd reached his destination in record time, hoping for good news. Alas, his hopes were dashed the moment he glimpsed the concerned, strained face of this good man who had maintained such cordial relations with all the religious groups working for the well-being of the country.

"The news is not good, I fear," the Bible Society head stated sadly. "I have had to renounce my own citizenship and adopt the citizenship of this country in order to keep the society running. If I go, it will close forever, I am afraid."

Going on, he said, "Several more Catholic priests have just been expelled. The Anglican Archbishop has gone. The Assembly of God

Church held a council, and on the very next day all their expatriate workers flew home.''

Pastor Silva would find out later, in prison, that the action of this particular group had aroused the suspicions of the authorities, and they were determined that no others would be allowed to leave. From now on, it would be ''IMPRISON HIM!'' when a preacher was brought in. At that point, mercifully, he did not know this.

After these two dedicated Christian men prayed together, Pastor Silva drove back to his office. On the way his spirits, which had been much downcast as a result of what he had been told, lifted. Some glorious texts ran through his mind. ''Fear thou not, for I am with thee; be not dismayed, for I am thy God.'' He said to himself, The Lord is going to take care of us. The Adventist people have a very special task to perform. We are here to warn this country of the soon coming of our Saviour. We will continue to do this.

But as he drove into the yard of the office, the publishing secretary's son met him, obviously much agitated.

''Pastor Silva,'' he burst out, ''I just had the strangest conversation with my father on the phone. He said he was calling from the Criminal Investigation Police Headquarters. First he mentioned that he wanted me to come to see him down there, and then later he said, 'No, no, don't come down here under any circumstances.' ''

''Son, I'll get to the bottom of this immediately,'' Pastor Silva told the young man. ''Try not to worry.''

But before he could sort out his thoughts and decide on a course of action, his secretary met him at the door.

''Pastor Silva,'' she told him, trembling, ''while you were gone a car drove up—not a police car, but a plain car, and three men got out. They said they were civil policemen. They demanded to see you. One of them was holding a paper in his hand that had your name on it. It also had our publishing secretary's name and our treasurer's name, but none of the first names matched the last names.''

(Later, in prison, Pastor Silva would learn that when these names had been forced out of the young imprisoned colporteur, he had tried to protect his leaders as best he could by mixing their names. A pitiful ruse, and he had been sick with sorrow for identifying them at all. But human flesh can endure only so much.)

Reassuring his secretary as best he could, Pastor Silva went into his office, closed the door, and sat down to think the most serious thoughts of his lifetime. Questions whirled in his mind endlessly.

What was the objective of the criminal police? Were his two colleagues even now being held in the police station? How had they obtained permission for the telephone call? Should he go immediately to the police station and place himself also in jeopardy?

In the midst of his mental and emotional turmoil his treasurer knocked at his door. Quickly Pastor Silva gave him a rundown on the events of the morning.

"I've been sitting here thinking," he said, "and I can see only one course of action open to me. I cannot abandon my workers down there in the Criminal Investigation Building. Neither can I plan my own escape, not knowing what has happened to them, though for the sake of my family that would probably be a wise move."

A shadow drifted over his face as he thought of the beloved three. But Elena had always shared all his ministry and his convictions. He knew that she would not want him to do less than his best, no matter what it might cost. But then practical considerations took over. He glanced at the calendar.

"It's very near the end of the month," he said, "and you know we're always a bit short financially at that time. If there should be any delay in my return from the Criminal Investigation Building, would you please see that Elena has a cash advance?"

Almost tearfully, the treasurer agreed. Their salaries were all so low that making them stretch throughout the entire month was a real feat—to say nothing of the problem of galloping inflation which ate up their meager funds like an insatiable monster.

Seeing that the treasurer was really anguished with concern for him, Pastor Silva rose and put his hand on his colleague's shoulder. "Don't worry," he told his friend. "After all, I am a Brazilian, and that fact will carry a lot of weight. This government doesn't want to get into a big argument over mistreatment of one of Brazil's citizens."

His words had the desired effect. The treasurer looked less downcast, less hopeless. Pastor Silva only wished that his own words had reassured himself as much.

The moment he had been dreading had come. He must go up the stairs, open the door to his apartment, and tell Elena what had happened and what he was about to do. As he entered the living room, he could hear her in the kitchen, preparing lunch. "Elena," he said, standing in the kitchen doorway, "could I talk to you for just a minute?"

One quick glance at his face convinced her that something very serious was in the air. Turning off the stove and washing her hands, she came to him. Quickly he outlined the events of the morning, leaving out nothing.

Her face was pale when he finished, but she said little. "Dearest, let's go to our room, kneel beside our bed, and pray for wisdom and for God's protection," he suggested. This was their custom in time of special need. Both arose from their knees refreshed spiritually and filled with a kind of desperate courage.

"Let's not say anything to the girls yet," Pastor Silva told her. "Everything just may work out beautifully. We don't have to worry them unnecessarily." He remembered that when they as parents had had to tell the girls that they must never walk on the streets without an adult, this had been a blow; he disliked making them more apprehensive than they already were.

Elena agreed. Then, though lunch, their large meal of the day, wasn't ready, she quickly prepared a plate for him, and he sat down to eat. He had told her that he wasn't hungry—that he wondered, in fact, if he could choke down any food. But she had begged him to eat, reminding him that he might need all his strength for whatever was ahead.

He ate only a few mouthfuls. On the hard prison floor, hungry now, and not knowing when he would ever be given food again, Pastor Silva almost wept at the thought of that last meal in his home. Moreover, as he thought of the pretty bedroom and the rest of the apartment, he was almost in despair.

When he was ready to leave for the Criminal Investigation Building, by unspoken common consent he and Elena had told one another good-bye in an almost casual manner. They hadn't made anything special over it. With their emotions so close to the surface and fear so overwhelming in their hearts, if they had indulged themselves in an emotional farewell, the damage to their nerves would have been enormous. So they simply pretended that Pastor Silva was going downtown on an errand, as he so often did.

When he walked away, he glanced back at the building which housed so much that was dear to him—Elena and Maria and Lucila, and the mission headquarters. Then he walked on rapidly for about one kilometer. He had decided that it would be best for him not to take the car, since the future was so uncertain. Briskly he strode down the wide street flooded with sunshine. The dreaded Criminal Investigation Building loomed up ahead of him. Standing in the bright, warm sunshine, he shivered in spite of the heat.

Just then, with only about a fourth of a block to go, he spotted a car that seemed very familiar. Yes, it was the publishing secretary's car. Somehow it seemed forlorn, as though its owner would never be coming back. Pastor Silva pushed such thoughts away resolutely. He took a small piece of paper from his notebook, wrote on it that he had been there, and stuck it under the windshield wiper.

All too well he knew that people could disappear without a trace. If this should be his fate, then the note would alert his friends to the fact that he had at least come this far.

Great crowds of people were gathered on the steps in front of the tall building. They always were. It was rumored that they waited— and waited—and waited—for news of their loved ones who had gone inside. Just inside the door, Pastor Silva found nothing but confusion. People were milling about. Should not there be a receptionist's desk near the entrance? Fearing to ask soldiers who stood in grim postures here and there, and fearing to call attention to himself in any way, he watched and observed and followed others down a long corridor. Then almost in surprise, he found himself in a room with his publishing secretary and the national pastor who had accompanied the secretary to the building.

"Why, there you are!" he greeted them, pretending not to notice the three or four policemen in the room. "Your wife is going to be very upset with you. Don't you know that it's already past twelve o'clock and your lunch is ready at home?"

The two of them gazed at him almost as though he weren't there. What could have happened to cause them to act so strangely? He decided to pretend, however, that everything was completely normal and to continue ignoring the policemen who, he felt sure, were in the room for the sole purpose of watching the two ministers.

Sitting down in a chair beside the two men, he suggested, "Now tell me all about the morning."

Still they were reluctant to talk. His publishing secretary's face was flushed and tense. Neither man could seem to meet his eyes fully. They seemed unable to concentrate. Finally the publishing secretary replied, haltingly, that they had been in an office on the second floor, but had been brought down to the first floor to wait during the lunch hour until two o'clock, when the police inspector would resume his interrogation.

"Well, then, you should be having your lunch also," Pastor Silva informed them loudly, for the benefit of the listening and watching policemen. "I'm sure that was the inspector's plan. No one is expected to do without his lunch."

Pausing for a moment, as if to think, he spoke as though a sudden inspiration had just occurred to him.

"Look—there's a little snack bar right down the street. Why don't the three of us go there and have lunch? We can be back here by two o'clock."

Out of the corner of his eye he watched the face of the policeman who seemed to be in charge. What would be his reaction? Would this suggestion cause all three of them to be tied to their chairs?

To his surprise and relief, it seemed to him that no negative expression crossed the face of the officer. It almost seemed as though he would do nothing to stop the three of them if, with no fanfare or apparent nervousness, they left the room.

Pastor Silva's facile brain had been working at lightning speed. He reasoned to himself that if he could get the two ministers outside where they could talk freely, and if he ascertained that indeed his suspicions were correct—that they were in custody—the three of them would run to the British embassy only a block and a half away. If they explained their desperate plight they would not, he felt sure, be denied asylum.

He felt as though every nerve in his body were shouting silently, "Come on! Come on! This may be our last chance! Risk it! Risk it!"

With the two other men he was vividly aware of the guns in the holsters of the policemen, yet the latter made no move to touch the weapons. But his two companions sat as though graven in stone, almost as though hypnotized, their eyes fixed fearfully on the guards. They seemed almost not to be hearing his urgent pleas.

Then another gambit occurred to him. "I'm leaving now," he said to them loudly and firmly. "There's no point in staying here during the lunch hour. No business will be transacted. Come on. We'll get back in plenty of time."

When they merely continued to gaze at him with dull, frightened eyes, he walked from the room, feeling a trickle of icy sweat between his shoulder blades, wondering if the last sound he would hear on this earth would be a bullet.

But nothing happened. Unbelievingly, he walked out the door, through the packed corridor, down the steps, and into the street. Never had the air seemed so sweet. He gulped in great lungfuls, the release of pressure so great that he felt almost faint. But he also felt confused and disoriented. Perspiring copiously, he started to walk in one direction. Then, with no conscious decision, he turned and walked in another direction. Once more he passed the publishing secretary's car, and he left another little paper on the windshield, noting only the time. At least there would be some sort of record of where he had been during the afternoon. (Much later he would learn that his notes had been found by the publishing secretary's son.)

He carried on a conversation with himself—a conversation which raged back and forth like a storm. "I could go on back to my home now, and I think I would have no further difficulty with the police," he said to himself. "They didn't indicate that they were interested in me."

But even as the thought came to him, he rejected it. When he had accepted the post of leader of the work in this sad country, he had made a full commitment. To Pastor Silva this meant that his place must be at the side of his workers who were now in such great jeopardy. Even his adored Elena and Maria and Lucila, whom he thought of with anguish, must not sway his purpose. And so, with dragging steps, he turned and went into the sinister building once more.

Entering the now-familiar room, he found that his two workers had barely moved. They sat motionless. They seemed unable to answer his low-voiced questions. Again, though, he had the strong impression that the police guard would not stop the three of them if they "went out for lunch." With all the force at his command, he almost orderd the two other men to "come with me." But they could not. He felt that if he left the room, they might perhaps have the courage to follow him—but they didn't.

Out in the street again, and now almost disoriented by the force of his emotions and the gravity of what might lie ahead, he breathed one silent prayer after another. Just where did his duty lie? It had seemed so clear only a few moments ago. Then, though he hadn't thought of it for years, a story which he had read in the *Review and Herald* during his impressionable years came into his mind with such clarity that he felt as though a giant television screen were in front of him with words being projected onto it.

"Two alpinists," the story went, "were climbing a very high peak. They were tied to one another by a stout rope, for safety's sake. Suddenly one of them began to fall. His companion saw what was happening, whipped out his knife, and cut himself loose. He was saved—but his companion, whom he might have saved, fell to instant death hundreds of feet below.''

Pastor Silva said to himself, Could I do that? Could I cut myself free and let these two fine men fall to whatever fate awaits them, when my presence might make a difference? And suddenly he remembered that his publishing secretary had left his Brazilian homeland and had come to this strange country because *he*, Antonio Silva, had suggested it and placed the call for his services. No, his decision was now irrevocable. He would go back and remain with his two workers, no matter what his or their fate would be.

This time he did not even attempt to coax them out of the room. He had begun to realize that the psychological ordeal and the pressures of the morning must have wrecked their will and drained all emotions. And so the three of them sat silently. Two o'clock came. Never had time so dragged on leaden feet.

The suspense was choking him. Suddenly the door was flung open. A uniformed man with a gun at his belt called the names of Pastor Silva's two workers.

"Come with me!" the guard ordered harshly.

As inconspicuously as he could, Pastor Silva followed and saw that when they entered the elevator, their guard pushed the button for the second floor. The elevator door closed before Pastor Silva had time to enter. But even so, he reasoned, it might be better for him to use another elevator. He arrived on the second floor just in time to see his workers and their guard walk down a long corridor and disappear behind a door. With his heart pounding like a hammer he followed them and opened the door.

There, sitting behind a huge and imposing desk was an equally huge and imposing black national man—the inspector. After calmly motioning for the three men to sit, he went back to studying a paper on his desk. As the silence deepened, Pastor Silva was sure that the heavy beating of his heart could be heard throughout the room. Surely almost anything would be better than this suspense.

At last the inspector spoke.

"Are all three of you pastors?" he demanded.

They answered affirmatively.

"Which one of you is in charge of the Seventh-day Adventist work in this country?" was his next question.

Taken by surprise, since up until this time he had considered himself only a spectator, Pastor Silva hesitated for a moment, then answered firmly, "I am in charge."

Without moving a muscle in his face or changing his expression in any way, the inspector turned to each of the other men and repeated the question.

"Pastor Silva is in charge," each answered. Only then did the inspector seem satisfied that the answer was true.

"Now," he demanded, turning specifically to Pastor Silva, "I want you to tell me the names of all the pamphlets which the Adventist Church distributes in this country."

Pastor Silva was momentarily staggered. How could he possibly remember the title of every pamphlet which the church used?

"Sir," he replied, "I will tell you as many titles as I can remember, but I would like to give you a full set of the materials. I could go to my office, get them, and bring them back in a short time."

The inspector brushed this suggestion aside. (Later, in prison, Pastor Silva would learn that the inspector had been referring to the cards which invited people to enroll in the Bible Correspondence School.)

After Pastor Silva had reeled off as many titles as he could remember, the inspector remarked curtly, "That's enough!" Then he turned to his phone and gave some orders in a native language to one of his assistants in another room. Soon a man whom Pastor Silva assumed to be the assistant entered. The inspector ordered, "Go with him!"

Not knowing what his destination was, and realizing that his two workers were not being allowed to accompany him, Pastor Silva momentarily panicked. But then his calm and confidence returned. He walked out of the room, followed by the minor official. They were met on the steps of the building by three policemen in civilian clothes and entered a waiting car.

The officer driving the car obviously knew his destination. In just a few minutes he pulled the car up in front of the mission headquarters. Pastor Silva was ordered to get out. Since it was Friday afternoon, the office was closed. He knew that Elena and the girls were in the third-floor apartment, however, and his fear for them knew no bounds. But somehow he managed to maintain a completely calm exterior, since he did not want the officers to mistake nervousness for guilty mannerisms.

How strange it felt to Pastor Silva to insert a key in the familiar lock

66

with the four officers close behind him. The quiet, deserted building
seemed almost like something from another planet. However, showing no hesitation, he strode down the corridor to the inner door of the
Book and Bible Shop and began collecting pamphlets and handing
them over to the inspector's assistant.

"I want some of your magazines and your books also," the official
demanded.

Pastor Silva was happy to comply. He included *The Great Con-
troversy* and *The Desire of Ages,* feeling that possibly some good
might come out of this terrible Friday after all.

Impatiently, though, the official now began to riffle through the
carefully-stacked shelves, snatching at this and that. He seemed
particularly interested in a booklet on the topic of Jehovah's
Witnesses. Then his attention was captured by a book about tithe-
paying. Pastor Silva's heart began to sink, for the Jehovah's
Witnesses were hated intensely by the government. Thousands of
them already had been imprisoned. As for tithing, this had been
declared an "imperialistic ruse" to take money out of the country.
The people had been told that tithing was exploitation, nothing more
nor less.

During these stressful minutes, two thoughts had been uppermost
in Pastor Silva's mind. One, that Elena and Maria and Lucila must not
be arrested and two, that the officer must not enter the treasury office.
Were they to enter this office, he was sure that they would interpret
the financial records as subversive. Then everyone connected with
the mission, no matter how trivial his job, would be imprisoned.
Inconspicuously, he tried to stand in front of the door marked
"Treasury" thus screening the words from the view of the searchers.

"Please, Lord, blind their eyes to this room" Antonio Silva prayed
in his extremity.

The Lord did. Somehow it never seemed to dawn on the searchers
that the other rooms led to other offices. Even now, on this first night
of his imprisonment, Pastor Silva was grateful as he realized that he
had had the presence of mind to do all he could to protect the others.
He thanked the Lord for having blessed his efforts in that respect.

To his horror, just as the search was nearly ended, Elena came
down the stairs. She had seen the car pull up in front of the building
and had seen Antonio, guarded by the four men, enter the mission. It
was not her way to run and hide. She must see what was happening
and deal with it. With her eyes he sent her eloquent messages,

eloquent signals. "Go back upstairs!" "Go back upstairs!" his eyes pleaded. She grasped his meaning. She stood for moment to allay the suspicions of the police, then turned, and with the heaviest heart of her life, retraced her steps.

Antonio couldn't know that this was the last time for many months that he would, as a free man, see his wife.

(Later, after the ordeal was over, he would learn from Elena that on several occasions the police went from house to house, searching every room with the most minute care. To the astonishment of the workers left in the mission building, the soldiers never came again to their door. This did not, however, alleviate the tension they felt each time they saw the familiar police cars draw up to the nearby houses.)

Carrying the pamphlets and books they had been given, plus those they had grabbed, the guards hustled Pastor Silva back into the car and drove rapidly to the Criminal Investigation Building. They hurried him into the now all-too-familiar office of the inspector, piled the printed matter on his desk, and left the room.

Pastor Silva's two workers were still sitting there, still silent, still wrapped in ominous thought. Painstakingly the inspector began to go through the material page by page. Is he a slow reader? wondered Pastor Silva, as the minutes ticked by, then the hours. Once in awhile the inspector would toss out a question in a desultory manner, as though the answer really wasn't important, but that for the sake of "form" he asked it.

Now it was five o'clock on Friday afternoon.

"If we don't get this matter cleared up soon, I won't be able to have my bath and be ready for Sabbath," Pastor Silva thought to himself. Ever since he had become involved in this macabre charade, he had gravitated between thinking that soon he would be released (after all, it was totally irrational to consider anything else) and an icy premonition that he would be taken into custody. He had prayed earnestly during the day for God's protection and deliverance. But he had also prayed for strength and courage to meet whatever might come.

Suddenly the inspector closed the book he had been scrutinizing, pushed the pamphlets aside, rolled a sheet of paper into his typewriter, and began to type with two fingers.

"Give me your full name!" he commanded Pastor Silva. Then "Country of Origin" and "Birthdate" and other routine items. He repeated the process with the other two pastors. They were now exchanging glances of real alarm. Was this . . . ? Could this . . . ?

68

"Stand up!" he suddenly barked.

Startled, they obeyed.

"Now empty your pockets and place everything on my desk," he ordered.

With a sinking heart, Pastor Silva realized that this man intended to imprison the three of them—without giving them an opportunity to speak in their own defense. For that matter, he was going to imprison them without even telling them their "crime."

Realizing all this, Pastor Silva took courage in his hands and asked, "May I say a few words, Sir?"

Grudgingly the large inspector nodded permission.

"Mr. Inspector," Pastor Silva said earnestly, "we two are Brazilian citizens. We were called by the people of your country to work for the betterment of conditions here. I am sure that you have a family of your own, so you will understand how hard it was for us to leave all our dear ones and come so far away from them. But we were happy to do it, for we felt that we could help the people of your lovely country."

The inspector listened impassively, no flicker of expression crossing his face.

With a silent prayer that God would send him the right words, the most effective words, Pastor Silva continued.

"We have over 8000 students in out-schools who are learning to read and write. Think what an asset these students will be to your government. Not only that, but in our medical work we are trying to teach your people about correct diet and good living habits so that your nation can be healthier and happier."

His heart sinking, Pastor Silva began to realize that the inspector had decided from the beginning what his course of action would be and that the afternoon of "examination" had been a mere sham. Nothing he said would make any difference.

Frantically then, the publishing secretary asked to speak. The inspector let him talk for only a few seconds, then cut him off. But Pastor Silva was not yet prepared to go down to defeat.

Courteously he inquired, "Then may I speak with your superior?"

"I am obeying orders; I am doing what I have been told to do," the inspector replied icily. "There is no need for you to bother any other person in this building with your foolish talk."

As Pastor Silva drew in his breath, preparing to insist, the inspector barked, "This interview is over! Be silent!"

The three of them stood there in the saddest silence of their lives as their jailer put their watches, papers, wallets, and all their other possessions in large envelopes and marked their names on the outside. Then he called one of the policemen into the room.

"Take them down!" he ordered. Pastor Silva knew what he meant. He meant—"Imprison them!"

Motioning with his rifle butt, the policeman herded the three men down to the first floor, where about twenty other prisoners were waiting. As he saw the coarse features of these men, the record of brutality on the faces of so many, Pastor Silva's heart sank even further. Surely even this blind government could not be so heartless as to lump together educated, innocent men with tough street criminals. The latter, who might already have committed murder, would have no compunctions about murdering their cellmates. What if they were drug users? He pushed these terrifying thoughts out of his mind.

In his shock and confusion, Pastor Silva had not even considered how he and the other men would be transported to the prison. Now, to his horror, as the guards formed them into small groups, he realized that they were going to be marched through the main street of the city, across town to the prison.

When they were down the steps and on the sidewalk, groups of people stopped to stare—some fearfully—afraid that they might one day meet a similar fate. Most people, though, sneered at the prisoners, obviously taking the position that they heartily deserved what they were getting. Every fiber of Pastor Silva's body shrank in agony. His self-respect seemed totally destroyed. All the years of biblical training, the high ideals, the dedication to humanity, the personal grooming—in one instant, all seemed swept away by the decision of a mindless official whose only claim to authority was the brutality of violent revolution.

In those first moments, he felt crushed to nothingness. Faintly, through the buzzing in his ears, he remembered Christ's walk through Jerusalem with His heavy cross. Was he not able to follow his Lord, even in this darkest of hours? He fastened his thoughts on his home— the one sane place in a world gone suddenly mad. It was sundown. Elena and Maria and Lucila would be waiting for him, waiting for the husband and father who would not come. The Bibles would be ready. The hymnals would be ready. Every Friday night there was singing, scripture reading, and comforting prayers. Then, a simple meal around the table, the four of them rejoicing in each other.

What will this Friday evening be like for my little family? he asked himself. He prayed that God would bring comfort and courage to their hearts.

Then the great prison complex loomed ahead. Even now, hours later, as he lay in the cell, Pastor Silva thought he would never forget his first sight of these buildings—as a prisoner. The complex occupied an entire city block, with walls about three meters high. Inside the heavily guarded walls one building housed the soldiers who acted as guards, another building contained administrative offices, and another functioned as a garage and repair shop for the prison vehicles.

The prison itself, enormous and menacing, was composed of two floors and a basement, but Pastor Silva's mind was now occupied with more pressing thoughts than where he and his two companions would be incarcerated.

As carefully and inconspicuously as possible, he drew close to the publishing secretary. In the lightest of whispers he said, ''We must do something to warn the others at the mission and also let them know what has become of us.'' The publishing secretary gave a faint nod of agreement.

Just then they reached the office of the prison commander. Each man was required to state his name. This was written down in a book by an assistant to the commander.

''Remove your belts, ties, and pens or pencils!'' barked a guard.

Somehow the whole scene had taken on an air of unreality to Pastor Silva. How could this be happening? How could it be possible that he, a college graduate, an ordained minister, a leader of scores of workers, a believer in God, and up until a few hours ago, a free man, was now here? He resolved that he would not disappear into this giant complex without a trace.

Edging his way to the desk, he spoke to the prison commander with courtesy and deference.

''Sir, may I make just one telephone call to my wife? She is not aware of what has happened.''

''PRISONERS DON'T MAKE TELEPHONE CALLS!'' was the shouted reply. ''STAND BACK!''

And then Pastor Silva finally realized, with sick despair, that he no longer had any rights. He was barely a number; no longer a person.

Yet one more idea occurred to Pastor Silva as the rest of the prisoners were being entered in the prison book. He had been scrutinizing the guards stationed at various places in the room. Somehow the countenance of one of them seemed different than the others. The guard seemed kinder, less grim, less hostile. Breathing a prayer, Pastor Silva edged his way toward the guard. When he was near, and after ascertaining that no one was watching, he whispered, almost without moving his lips, ''Would you telephone my wife for me? She does not know I am a prisoner.''

The guard said not one word in reply. Nodding, he took out his pen and a little notebook. Grasping that this gesture meant compliance, Pastor Silva whispered his phone number. The guard wrote it down.

''And just one more thing—oh, if you would only be so kind— would you tell my wife to tell Da Cunha to take the little daughter to a physician anywhere one may be found? If not in this country, then in Swaziland or South Africa.''

Again the guard nodded his agreement. The message, of course, was a prearranged code. To take a relative somewhere meant that all should escape if possible. ''Da Cunha'' was the name of the treasurer; Pastor Silva now knew that the police already had the former's name and feared that he would be the next to be arrested. He was sending the only warning possible, but it was enough.

(Much later, after his imprisonment, he learned that the guard had indeed phoned Elena as promised; in fact, when he phoned on Friday night Elena and the girls were not at home; they were on a frantic search for Pastor Silva. The guard actually phoned again on Saturday to be sure the message was received. Can even prison guards be angels unawares? In later years Antonio was to think of this guard many times. The warning to Pastor Da Cunha got through also; he had been negotiating for an air ticket to fly out of the country to attend year-end division meetings. He had his ticket and his visa in hand. With these documents he had no difficulty in securing tickets for his family also. Therefore, the entire family escaped in the next few days. Very soon after he left, the police broke into his apartment and searched it exhaustively. Then they moved all his possessions. Officially, though, he had not run away, because he had legally left the country with his family, using bona fide air tickets and visas.)

Lying on the cell floor, cold, cramped, hungry, miserable, and afraid, Pastor Silva kept remembering the events of the preceding day. When he had given his messages to the guard, his next fear was that he would be put into a cell separated from his two companions. ''Oh, Lord,'' he prayed silently, ''please don't let this happen. Let us stay together so that we can be a strength to one another.''

With profound gratitude then, he had discovered that the three of them were being pushed into the crowded cell together. In the milling, raging mob, they had soon identified the young colporteur. When he saw them, he wept.

"Dear, dear pastors!" he sobbed. "I cannot believe that we are here in this terrible place. Our freedom is gone. I am afraid that I am responsible for your arrest. I am so sorry. I am so sorry."

In trying to comfort him, their own hearts were somewhat warmed. Then, having spent most of the night reviewing the events of recent days and years, Pastor Silva's exhausted mind and body gave out. He drifted into a light sleep just before dawn, into welcome oblivion for an hour or two.

Enduring
the Unendurable

At 6:00 a.m. Pastor Silva heard the sounds of shouted commands from those whom the prisoners had chosen as their leaders. For a moment his tired mind could not, however, grasp where he was. But it was not a horrible nightmare. He watched as all the prisoners struggled to their feet and pressed themselves together on one side of the cell as tightly as they could. What is going to happen? he wondered, with his heart thudding heavily.

It was almost anticlimactic to discover that this was the beginning of the daily clean-up ritual, which would continue for all the months he was in prison. Each morning several prisoners were chosen to take pieces of old blankets, dip them in the only available water at the other end of the cell, and drag these wet rags along the floor. Then all the prisoners moved to the other side. They pressed together, as the wet rags were dragged across the opposite floor. Pastor Silva never learned whether this had been commanded by the jailers or whether it was a system that the prisoners themselves had thought up.

"Breakfast!" shouted the guards. Pastor Silva and his companions were ravenous by now, having had almost nothing to eat during the preceding day. All the prisoners were shoved into a line and taken single file to a dining room about ten meters from the cell. In the room were cement tables and seats about three-and-one-half meters long. Ten persons had to sit on each side of each table, pressed tightly together.

"What's this stuff?" the publishing secretary whispered to Pastor Silva, as some muddy brown liquid in old, dirty, misshapen aluminum vessels was passed around.

"Maybe it's coffee," was the reply.

Patiently, they waited. But their hopes were dashed when the only other item on the menu was a piece of bread about half the size of a man's hand, with a minute portion of jam smeared on it.

"I must take very small bites so that I will feel that I have had more food," Pastor Silva told himself. But he was so hungry that he almost wolfed the bread down. Later he would learn that this first hunger, immediately after having been well-nourished, would not compare with the desperate hunger that he would develop—a hunger that tortured him day and night.

Back in the cell, the three pastors sought out the young colporteur and talked with him. "Actually, many of the men in this cell are not bad people," he told them. "I have found that some of the nearly 140 are religious people, and that is the only reason they are here. We do not need to fear anything from them. We need fear only the actual criminals."

Though nothing at this point could provide much comfort, at least this small ray of light was a help. Then Pastor Silva asked a question which he could not hold back.

"During the time you have been here, has any religious captive been released?"

Sadly the young colporteur shook his head, "No."

As the conversation progressed, Pastor Silva could see that the young man was distraught and uneasy. He sensed the reason. "Please don't think that we hold you responsible for our imprisonment," he told the colporteur. "These things happen. God will see all of us through."

Pastor Silva felt a lump in his throat. He had studied with this young man and had prepared him for baptism. He felt a great affection for him. Why should the two of them, innocent as they were, be in this terrible place? Only one comfort remained—that the Adventist truth had transcended racial and color barriers. The two white pastors, the young black colporteur, and the black national pastor were united in perfect love and brotherhood in their terrible circumstances.

Throwing his arms around Pastor Silva, the young colporteur wept. "When the interrogators demanded the names of the leaders of our work here, I tried not to answer, but they have ways of getting the information they want. I mixed up your first and last names, hoping that would give you extra time," he choked.

"So that's how it happened," Pastor Silva said to himself, remembering the confusion over names in the office on the preceding day.

Sadly, the colporteur related another incident that happened on that momentous Friday. While he was being interrogated by the inspector, an assistant had come into the room and announced that two pastors were downstairs and wished to talk to the inspector. (At that time the colporteur did not know that the pastors were working in his behalf.)

The inspector, through clenched teeth, had grated, "Ah, they are PASTORS! Then I shall imprison them!"

The colporteur knew that it would be fatal to protest such injustice. And through the months of imprisonment, Pastor Silva was never told what his "crime" had been; he was never told why he was there. He was a pastor. That was sufficient crime.

The conversation with the young colporteur at an end, Pastor Silva began to realize how exhausted he was and what a toll the strain of the previous day had taken. Yet he could find no place to lie down—no place to stretch out. Over and over his tired mind kept repeating the words, It's Sabbath. It's Sabbath. I should be in church with my family. Why am I here?

He did not, though, give in to despair. As he crouched against the wall, dirty, disheveled, with no comb, no toothbrush, no washcloth, he tried to reason it all out. I am sure that I will hear my name called any minute and be taken off for a hearing, he said to himself. My people in the mission will be working feverishly for my release. Why, it's even possible that I'll be back home before Sabbath is over!

But he wasn't.

During the morning as the new prisoners were brought into the cell, further cramming the already packed room, if the prisoner were white, a shout would go up from the blacks. This shout was the rough equivalent of the English word, "Score!" Pastor Silva remembered that this shout had sounded when he and his two companions had entered the cell. What was it all about? Quietly he asked the young colporteur.

At first the latter was reluctant to reply. "Please don't feel bad, Pastor," he begged. "I must tell you that the people have been taught to think that all white people are their enemies. Even though we are all in this cell together, some of the blacks are happy to see as many whites thrown in as possible. In other words, it is one more 'score' for the black man."

How strange it seemed. All these men had been created in God's image. They had all come to a common fate in this hopeless place.

How could color still matter? Sadly he wished for a new heaven and a new earth, where nothing would matter but Christ and His love. This now seemed very far away.

Throughout the morning, Pastor Silva so wished for freedom that he became almost convinced that a guard would unlock the door and call his name. Then he would go for his hearing and be set free. After all, he had committed no crime. If the other pastors were not freed at the same time, he would bend every effort and every nerve to secure their release. He would work tirelessly for the young national colporteur also.

He spoke to one of the other prisoners, expressing his hope for release. The man looked at him impassively. ''Hope all you want,'' he said, ''but if you're not called before lunch, there will be no hope until Monday morning. The police inspectors don't work from Saturday noon until Monday morning.''

For the first time, an attack of sheer panic engulfed Pastor Silva. His heart beat wildly; he broke out in perspiration from head to foot.

''I can't stay in this cell another night,'' his mind silently screamed. ''I am choking. I am smothering with the loss of my freedom. Help me, Lord!'' His prayer was answered by a calming of his nerves. A kind of peace pervaded his being. He could face what must be faced.

But the relief of this calm period was short-lived.

Another refrain suddenly invaded his troubled thoughts. What have I done to my family? What have I done to those I love? The words repeated themselves, over and over. When I married Elena, I promised to love and protect her all the days of her life. Now I have led her into deadly danger. I have deprived her of her husband. I have brought her to a strange and hostile land. And my little girls—he almost wept aloud as he thought of them, so vulnerable without the protection of a father. For how long?

Then thoughts that he had pushed to the back of consciousness now crowded forward: his aged, frail father, who had suffered so much in the old country, and who needed Antonio to be a strength and comfort in his last years; his mother—his dear, dear mother—whose fear had overcome her when she had known that he would return to this strange land despite the danger. Her pleas for him to remain in his homeland rang in his ears so clearly that he almost clapped his hands against his head to shut them out.

''Lord, help me!'' was his frantic plea. His cry, soundless though it was, did not go unanswered. Again a wave of reassurance and peace washed over him. "Fear thou not; for I am with thee: be not dismayed; for I am thy God: I will strengthen thee; yea, I will help thee; yea, I will uphold thee with the right hand of my righteousness." The beautiful words—words which he had used so many times in sermons—came to him on angel wings.

During the Sabbath morning, while he was straining every nerve and muscle in hopes of release, more and more prisoners had been squeezed into the cell. He wondered how they could all stand, let alone lie down during the long night. When lunchtime came and went and he was still a prisoner, he began to look around more carefully. He must find out all he could about this dreadful place which was, for the moment, his only "home."

As he and the other three Adventists talked it over, they estimated that the cell was a little over five meters wide and 14 meters long, giving a total area of about 72 square meters (85 square yards). Sometimes ignorance is to be preferred to knowledge; thus it was good that Pastor Silva did not then know that this cramped area would eventually hold more than 200 men. His feeling of suffocation was already almost overwhelming. As his eyes roamed from wall to wall, he discovered that the cement floor and the brick and composition walls held nothing of interest. Physical needs were cared for behind a small wall at one side, with a water faucet and a hole in the corner. This was the entire provision for personal hygiene for the 140, and later 200, men in the cell.

When he expressed his feelings of near-panic and deplored the tiny cell packed with all kinds of men—a few good, but many totally evil—the young colporteur answered, "But Pastor, we are lucky to be in this cell. Don't you see that it has windows? It's a corner cell with windows on two sides."

Pastor Silva looked at the cell again. It did indeed have eight big windows without glass, about one meter wide and two meters high, filled with strong, vertical iron bars.

"Look," one of his companions said. "From some of these windows we can see what's going on in the inner prison yard. And from the front window we can see who comes in and who goes out of the prison. From this other one we can see other cells and the dining room. We can even see the steps going up to the prison commander's office. Maybe we won't feel so terribly shut up if we can get a chance to look out of the windows several times a day."

Pastor Silva wondered how they would ever get near the windows.

Some of the other prisoners had apparently taken up permanent positions there.

Rain, wind, and dust poured through the windows as weather patterns changed. But the four Adventist prisoners were thankful for the continual fresh air. The stench of so many unwashed bodies and the incredibly inadequate sanitary facility would have been over-powering in a totally closed room.

As that Sabbath afternoon wore on, the four men tried to strengthen and comfort one another. Just when they needed it most, something happened that showed they were not forgotten. How, Pastor Silva never knew, but the publishing secretary's wife secured permission to enter the prison yard. She begged and begged until one of the guards agreed to bring her husband a small towel and a piece of soap. When the guard appeared in the cell and roughly shouted the secretary's name, the four companions were speechless. Nothing had ever seemed more precious than the soap and towel. They gazed at these objects almost in awe. They represented sanity. They represented the personhood of all free men who can keep their bodies clean and fresh and make their own decisions. For a few brief moments the panic and horror receded.

But the long, hot tropical afternoon stretched on and on. There was absolutely nothing to do. Pastor Silva's thoughts, dark and troubled, ran in many directions. Why did I ever complain to myself that I had more than I could do? he wondered. Why don't people in the "real" world understand that work is the greatest blessing of all? And as for the Sabbath—did I ever in my wildest imaginings picture myself in such a place on God's holy day? He thought again and again of the gracious Sabbath dinner table that his Elena always set. The fresh flowers, the daintily-prepared food, and most of all, the warmth and love of his family as they surrounded the table. Often guests shared the hospitality of their home.

He thought of the Sabbaths of his childhood and youth. At times there had not been much food but always more than enough love for God and love for one another to make the Sabbath special. He remembered the Sabbaths when he was a student in São Paulo and the special meal which was always served in the dining room.

All these past Sabbaths seemed very far away and unreal.

In the gathering darkness, lighted again by only the two small bulbs high in the ceiling, the prisoners, frustrated from the long day of inactivity, tried to begin settling themselves for sleep. On the night before, Pastor Silva had been almost too stunned to be fully aware of the true situation. Now he began to realize what it really meant to be incarcerated within a room filled with closely-packed humanity. His exhausted body demanded sleep. But how could he sleep in this place?

"You have to lie down on your sides," barked the "chief" of the cell. "Your back or chests cannot at any time touch the floor, or you will take more than your share of the floor," he commanded. This second night, when Pastor Silva and his companions positioned themselves on the floor, they found that the cell leaders, not satisfied, used their feet to kick and press the bodies closer together.

The feeling of claustrophobia became almost overpowering. But the Adventist men were grateful that their bodies touched mostly each other's bodies. They tried to keep a position near the wall to avoid contact with as many filthy bodies as possible. But it was a pathetic attempt.

No sooner had the cell appeared to be settling for the night than fights began to break out, probably because some wanted to sleep and some wanted to talk. Some men became so frustrated and angered by the lack of space that they began punching those on either side of them. Their victims retaliated. The fighting became so fierce that soldiers with clubs and guns finally had to come in and subdue the offenders. Watching all this, Pastor Silva thought, "They seem like wild animals. What will happen to us? We have been taught to turn the other cheek. Will we be killed by the other prisoners if not by the government?"

In spite of their determination to make the best of things and to survive, the crowded conditions on this second night became unendurable. They worked out a system whereby one of them would stand by the wall for an hour at a time in order to permit the others a few more inches of room. In this way they could stretch their cramped arms and legs and change positions slightly. This first Saturday night became typical of the nights which were to follow.

"I know now what the word 'nightmare' really means," Pastor Silva told his publishing secretary during the dawn hours of Sunday.

As he spoke, an unbidden thought came into his mind—the blue couch back in South America, with its comfort and cleanliness. His longing and nostalgia for the life which had been taken from him were so great that he thought his heart would stop in his chest.

The sharp pangs of hunger were beginning to be felt. But when the long line of men marched to breakfast, again they were given only the muddy brown liquid and half a slice of rough bread covered with a thin layer of jam. The cleaning of the cell had proceeded as on the Sabbath, with the men pressed into one side, while the designated few dragged the tattered wet blankets across the floor. Because some each night were incontinent and others vomited, the floor was filthy.

"If only I had something to read!" Pastor Silva said to his companions. "I truly did not realize how much time I spend reading, and how important a part of my life that is. To stand or crouch here with nothing to read and absolutely nothing to do is simply torture."

He asked the designated leaders if any books were available, and they laughed in his face.

"Something to read? Don't you know that prisoners are not allowed to read? You're cut off completely from the real world now. Forget it!"

But during the months of his imprisonment, the need for mental food was to Pastor Silva a nearly unendurable hunger.

He and his companions tried, as best they could, to have morning and evening worship. They repeated as many texts as possible, but sometimes it seemed to them that their minds were functioning very, very slowly.

Again, when hope seemed almost dead on that first Sunday morning, the other prisoners began murmuring and planning for "the afternoon visitation." "What are they talking about?" Pastor Silva asked his publishing secretary. But the latter was also mystified.

Overhearing their exchange of questions, a friendly prisoner said, "Why, didn't they tell you? Our relatives are allowed to come into the courtyard and talk to us through the bars for five minutes on Sunday and Thursday afternoons. They can come only from two o'clock to four o'clock, but it is better than nothing."

Pastor Silva's mind was whirling, trying to grasp this new development.

"Do they just come to the gate and ask the police to let them into the prison yard?" he asked.

"No, no, it's more complicated than that. In order to get permission, the family members must wait hours in the street. After a certain number have been let in, the rest are told that they will have to come back on the next visiting day."

Pastor Silva's thoughts raced with more questions. How would Elena know that such visits were even possible? Silently he prayed over and over, "Please, Lord, let Elena inquire about the possibility of visiting. Please impress this on her mind."

But he needn't have worried about Elena. She had been, he would later learn, tireless ever since his disappearance on Friday. She had learned everything she possibly could about the prison and what the prisoners were allowed. She had arisen very early, had awakened Maria and Lucila, and the three of them had gone to the prison. They had stood in the broiling tropical sun for hours. They had shown their identification papers, had been searched, and now, as two o'clock approached, they were let into the courtyard, their hearts beating hard. Would they actually see him? Was he there? Had the call from the friendly guard been a hoax?

Elena also had ascertained, with persistent questioning, that prisoners could receive clean clothes and small supplies if the relatives brought these items on the visits. The routine was this: she would approach a guard, hand the clean clothes to him, and tell him the name of the prisoner; then the guard would go to the cell, call the prisoner, hand over the clean clothes, receive the prisoner's dirty clothes, and at that point the prisoner was given permission to go to the iron-barred windows to "talk" with his relatives.

When the guard approached Pastor Silva with the latter's clean clothes, his surprise and joy were so great that quick tears sprang to his eyes. He was not forgotten! He could not wait to get to the window.

Alas, when he hurled himself through the tightly-packed bodies, receiving many threats and punches along the way, he discovered that the relatives were not allowed to come nearer than five meters. A grim line of soldiers stationed themselves at this distance to enforce the rule. At the windows so many prisoners were shouting and screaming messages that the din was indescribable. Frantically, knowing that he had only five minutes, Pastor Silva shouted to Elena, "Have you been in contact with the Brazilian government? Have you contacted the Adventist world headquarters in Washington, D.C.?"

But she could not hear him. Straining every nerve, she listened, in vain. Then she tried to shout questions at him, with the same result. Her strained, pale face went through him like a knife. He tried to smile reassurance and comfort to her, but somehow he knew that the smile did not appear as he wished it to.

"Elena, it may take a little while before I am released from here," he shouted in despair, thinking that this statement might cause her to be more resigned to his fate. He thought she had heard him, but he could not hear her reply. He could only see her lips moving.

Then, Pastor Silva's five minutes up, a guard harshly shoved him out of the way.

"Get back! Your turn is over!" the guard barked.

Standing on tiptoe as tall as possible, from his position at the back of the cell he caught one brief glimpse of Elena and Marie and Lucila slowly making their way out of the prison yard. They seemed to be waving their hands to him, over and over. Tears came again to his eyes as he realized that these three most dear of all on earth were suffering so keenly on his account. The little girls had been almost totally silent on this first visit, but their little faces told the story of their feelings.

As the weeks dragged by and turned into months, they began to live for the visits, sad though they were. One of the most agonizing features was the suspense. Although the family visitation was officially held on Sundays and Thursdays, the visits could be canceled at the whim of the police—and they often were. It was almost more than Pastor Silva and the others could endure, to live night and day for that five-minute period, only to find that it was canceled.

Each time he saw Elena and the girls, with the brief glimpses and the unsatisfactory exchange of attempted messages, it was harder to watch them disappear, always waving their hands until they were out of sight. Hardest of all were the times when Maria and Lucila could not control their tears. They would stand silently, the hot tears rolling down their cheeks, while he, their comforter and protector, was powerless to reach them. He would not learn until much later that the strain of the visits was so enormous that afterward, for hours, the three would walk the city streets, unable to remain still or to work at even simple home duties.

He had resolved at the first visit that the one thing he could do for his wife and daughters was to smile and to give an appearance of being cheerful. "They are bearing a heavy enough burden, without seeing me in despair," he told himself. From this resolve he was never shaken, no matter how somber his state of mind during the visitation times. Elena, too, had obviously made the same resolve, for she always presented him with a smile. Each was aware of the little game being played, but it was played out in love and regard for the feelings of the other.

Even with the unexpected visit from Elena and the girls, Pastor

Silva had existed in a state of almost suspended animation during that first Sunday. He had been told that the police office did no business on that day; nonetheless, the soul must have hope for its nourishment. He kept hoping and praying for a miracle. He still could not grasp the fact that a national of another country could be seized, his property taken from him, and be bodily thrown into prison without a trial and with no chance to hear the charges against himself. He could not grasp the reality of being dropped out of sight, with no recourse. No appeal.

The words, "Imprison him!" rang through his tired mind.

After another nearly sleepless night, he was wide awake long before the bulk of the prisoners stirred—groaning, complaining, some weeping, and some ill. He could not wait for Monday to come. Now, he told himself, his waiting would be at an end. When he had had prayer with the other Adventists before they tried to sleep, he had thanked God for the fact that they were all still alive; that they were not as yet ill. He thanked the Lord that tomorrow would be Monday.

"Surely we are bound to be called to the prison office, questioned, and released today," he assured them. He was not merely expressing optimism for the sake of his friends. He truly believed that this might be the case; that is, one part of his mind believed, but always there was the little nagging tug of apprehension.

The Monday morning routine was the same—the routine that seemed suddenly a part of his life. As he chewed on his small piece of bread, he thought of the amazing adaptability of the human being. The human spirit, when buoyed up by faith in God, can be exceedingly flexible. Nonetheless, he felt dirty and unkempt; he had no comb; his fingernails were already dirty; he was becoming a different person, one whom he barely knew.

After breakfast a guard opened the door of the cell and shouted a name. One of the prisoners jumped to his feet.

"Come with me!" the guard commanded. Stumbling in his haste to be out of the cell, the man complied. Later, though, he returned to the cell in despair. He had been interrogated again. He had not been released.

This was the pattern of the morning. Each time the door opened and a prisoner was called, Pastor Silva leaped to his feet, as did his three companions. Each time they hoped so desperately that their names would be called. They were straining every nerve. Yet it did not happen.

Most of the prisoners who were taken from the cell returned after a short time. Only three or four were released or taken to another prison. The prison "grapevine" could not always ascertain the fate of each man.

When Monday night came, with the dark shadows and the dim lights, Pastor Silva went through a period of discouragement so dark that for a time he could not find the face of God through the clouds. He had been so certain that he would be released—or at least given a hearing. He tried to sort out his mixed feelings—anger, frustration, hope, self-pity, self-condemnation. He was a human being, subject to all the conflicting emotions engendered during tragedy. Mentally he went over and over the events leading up to his imprisonment. He was tormented by a voice in his mind (Satan?) persistently whispering that "If you'd been more intelligent and had not come back to the Criminal Building the second time, you'd be a free man. Just look at what your devotion to so-called duty has done to you."

As these waves of negative feelings washed over him, he prayed, like a drowning man, "Lord, save me!" The Lord sent immediate feelings of peace into his troubled mind. But these negative emotions continued to recur and to harass him for several months, making his incarceration that much more difficult.

Nonetheless, after each bout with what he came to believe was Satan, he found comfort in examining his conduct, deciding that he could not have done differently no matter what the cost. At first one of his keenest regrets was that his companions had not accepted his invitation to lunch, at which time they could have run to the British Embassy for asylum. Later though, as the weeks passed and a kind of lasting peace filled his heart, he came to feel that it was all a part of God's plan. He explained this to the two pastors one day.

"If we had run away, this would have raised suspicion as to the loyalty of our national members in this country," he told them. "Perhaps many of them would have been arrested. Perhaps our own families would have been thrown into prison. So even though at the moment our fate is very hard, we can comfort ourselves with that thought."

He was careful not to indicate by any word or deed that he felt the two men had "let him down." They had not understood his plan; he had not been in a position to explain it to them; moreover, they had feared that if they left the building, they would be shot.

Hunger pangs had become so acute that the four of them kept visualizing their favorite foods—beautiful fruit salads, creamy rice, home-baked bread, cold milk, cold fruit juice, crisp crackers. Could all of these marvels actually exist just a few meters away on the other side of the wall?

Tuesday came—and he was called out of the cell! He had so longed for this moment that at first he could hardly recognize his own name.

"Antonio Silva!" the guard shouted again. "Come with me!"

He sprang to his feet. "If I am released now, I will immediately start proceedings for your release," he shouted to his three companions as he forced his way through the packed bodies to the cell door.

History seemed to be repeating itself. He was taken to the same office, to be interrogated by the same inspector who had commanded "Imprison him!" on the preceding Friday.

He was motioned to a chair and told to wait. To himself he thought, "One of the things you learn when you are a prisoner is to wait. Wait, wait, wait. This is hard. Througout his lifetime he had always been in a leadership role. Though he had never purposely kept anyone waiting if he could avoid it, he had always been "on the other side of the desk." He had always been "in charge." Now he was at the mercy of others.

Just when he thought his turn had come, a guard raced into the room and engaged the inspector in a quick conversation.

"A phone conversation is going on between a foreigner in his hotel room and someone in another country. Don't you want to hear it?"

Then Pastor Silva realized that what he had been told previous to his imprisonment was true. The new government had tapped the phones of all foreigners in the country. Whenever these particular phones rang, tapes were activated to record every word. With a sinking heart, he understood now that the phones at the mission had undoubtedly been tapped. He hoped with all his soul that nothing would be said on them to further jeopardize his safety or that of his three companions, to say nothing of his family and the other families.

The inspector did not return. With no explanation, a guard came to him and ordered him into another room. There, while continuing his interminable wait, he could see and hear other inspectors interrogating some of the Jehovah's Witnesses who had been taken into custody. He never would forget the questions these terrified people were asked, nor the manner in which they were asked—sneering, brutal, insensitive.

"So—you believe in God, do you?"

"Have you ever SEEN God?"

"Do you know where God lives?"

To one poor, trembling man an inspector shouted, "God is your conscience! Listen to it and obey our laws!"

Later Pastor Silva was told that a boy was sent back home by a policeman during interrogation while his father and mother were still being held in prison. When the boy, penniless, asked to be given a few cents to buy food, the answer was screamed at him, "Ask your God for the money!"

Sitting in the midst of this atmosphere, Pastor Silva thought of all the promises which had been made by the new government. "Freedom, liberty, and independence are for all," the people had been told over and over again. Never had there been the slightest hint that religion would be prohibited.

But in the inner workings of the government, as epitomized by the prison, how tragically different it all was. Pastor Silva, sitting in the interrogation room, suddenly remembered a sentence which was attributed to one of the army commanders: "The guns which have fought colonialism will now be turned against the religions in this country."

Listening to all these frightening interviews was not a calming experience for Pastor Silva. Knowing how important it was that he be in full command of himself, he prayed repeatedly for the strength of the Holy Spirit to be poured out on him in full measure.

Finally, about eleven o'clock, his interrogation began. Contemptuously the inspector threw trivial questions at him, questions which a child could have answered. But suddenly the tempo changed.

"Did you ever attend a meeting with ministers from the Church of God's Assembly?"

Pastor Silva answered that he had not done so.

"Do the workers and members of your church distribute pamphlets in the homes, in the streets, and in post office boxes?"

"Yes," answered Pastor Silva. "We have been offering material which will help your people lead a better life. But we did not distribute anything more after Independence Day."

The inspector snorted disbelievingly. Then came the questions which Pastor Silva now knew were the real keys to the situation—questions dealing with money.

"Do you have a tithe system in your church?" the inspector continued.

Pastor Silva knew that he must answer very carefully. But how could he open the mind of this rough, angry man and explain to him the entire beautiful system of Adventist giving?

"Yes," he answered slowly. He said nothing more, feeling that the fewer explanations he gave, the less chance there would be for the inspector to make accusations.

Coldly the inspector stared at Pastor Silva.

The interview seemed to be taking hours. He typed each answer onto a sheet of paper. Obviously he had had no training in typing, for he used two fingers in a laborious hunt-and-peck method.

Then the interrogation stretched on into further questions about Pastor Silva's direct responsibilities, how he had come to the country, how the whole system of ministers in the Adventist Church was arrived at. Each time a question was asked, Pastor Silva tried to answer correctly but to give nothing more than necessary. The inspector listened impassively. He continued to type with two fingers.

At last he ripped the sheet from the typewriter and handed the barely decipherable document over to Pastor Silva.

"Now read this, and read it carefully, so you will be sure when you sign it that these are the answers you gave."

As he read through the garbled page, Pastor Silva realized that the inspector had not typed all his answers. He had given no explanations. The material was really not accurate. What should he do? His mind was racing while his eyes were fastened on the page. He breathed another silent prayer for wisdom.

As if in direct answer to his prayer, the thought came to him: "If you don't sign, you may create a great deal more trouble—trouble which could mean a very bad situation for your family and for all the workers still at liberty here in this country. The inspector has not written down anything that is incorrect—he has simply not written down all you told him."

Pastor Silva glanced up. "I will sign," he declared.

The inspector handed him a pen.

It was done.

To the pastor's shocked surprise, the inspector then called one of the guards to take him back to the prison cell. His mind reeled. He had been sure that, after he signed the paper, he would be set free, or, in lieu of that, be given a full and complete hearing and then set free. As he walked back to his cell with dragging footsteps, he found himself again disoriented and unable to understand fully his situation. He still had not been accused of anything or told why he was a prisoner. He knew that it would do no good to demand an attorney. The new government had forbidden trials wherein prisoners could have legal representation. No lawyer was now permitted to have a private practice.

The walk back to the cell with the guard was one of the longest of his life. As the door clanged shut, he felt that now he was truly becoming a forgotten man, a man without rights and without a country. His three companions, who had also hoped and prayed desperately for his release, were equally shocked, equally disappointed. The four of them knelt together in a small corner, turning their backs on the rest of the prisoners. By now the prisoners had discovered that the four men were workers for God. A few had become friendly and trusting and seemed to derive comfort from staying as close as possible.

Wednesday dragged on leaden feet.

Thursday came and went, with a brief glimpse of Elena, Maria, and Lucila, and a change of underclothing.

Friday came. By now Pastor Silva and his three companions were so hungry and weak that they had to pray constantly just for physical strength to withstand whatever would be their fate. Pastor Silva struggled with feelings of such despair as he had never imagined possible. Was no one trying to arrange for his freedom? Would he die here?

The only way he could banish these destructive thoughts was by prayer. If only I had my Bible, he thought over and over again. If only I had some of Ellen White's books. He could remember many texts and precious promises, and passages from the spirit of prophecy, but he needed the comfort of seeing the words on the page in front of him.

On Friday afternoon the cell door clanged open, and the names of his three companions were called. They were to be interrogated. The pattern was somewhat the same as in Pastor Silva's interrogation, except for the treatment of the national pastor. To him the inspector was brutal, sneering, and threatening. At one point he shouted, "Do you think these foreigners would come to this country unless they expected to derive great benefits for themselves?"

"Yes," the national pastor answered softly, not knowing whether his answer might cause his death.

When the four were reunited in the cell, they discussed the philosophy behind the cruel question.

"You see," Pastor Silva said, "the people who have taken over this government simply cannot understand religious people who are willing to lose all their possessions and to be separated from their beloved relatives and go to a poor foreign country simply to help people. For them, the idea of preaching means political propaganda.''

"Yes,'' agreed the publishing secretary, ''they have been indoctrinated with the belief that various religions are tools of capitalism designed to tame the people in order to exploit them.''

Pastor Silva reminded them, ''We have read in the papers here that missionaries are agents of international capitalism.''

As the four of them sat for a while in silence, Pastor Silva wished that he could be sure missionaries of churches other than his own had always been circumspect in their actions. Well, there may have been a tiny grain of truth in the present accusations, though not, he was convinced, as far as the Adventists were concerned.

Starvation and Sickness

The second Sabbath was now to be spent in that terrible cell. Each night sleep came both harder and easier. The enormous frustration of inactivity each day, the lack of exercise and mental stimulation, produced such a high degree of tension that, at times, the four companions felt their nerves would snap completely. Yet their increasing weakness from lack of food coupled with their depression caused them to welcome the idea of sleep. For a brief period they could forget.

For the first seven or eight days of their imprisonment they were given the half piece of bread for breakfast, plus two other very scanty meals. They were never sure that the food was clean enough to eat. Avoiding germs in the cell was impossible. They could not keep themselves clean. Each time they were herded into the "dining room" for meals, Pastor Silva found the affront to his self-respect harder to bear. Was this to be his fate for the rest of whatever life remained to him? Did all the years of education and learning to live as a human being in the image of God count for nothing? Could everything that made him a man be wiped out so easily by a blind, uncaring force?

Just when it seemed as though he and his companions could endure nothing more, things became worse. One morning they were given their half slice of bread, as usual. The morning dragged along, the four of them in despair, trying to repeat all the Bible texts they could remember yet unable really to think of anything else but their gnawing physical hunger.

The noon hour came and went. They were given nothing to eat.

Even though Pastor Silva had dreaded the "dining room," where the prisoners, given no utensils, had to scoop up food with their fingers, he now longed for nourishment, any nourishment, under any conditions.

He approached one of the guards.

"Could you tell me when we will have our meal?" he asked courteously.

Angrily the guard shouted, "The steam system in the kitchen has broken down. No one knows how to repair it. You can blame this on yourself and the whites who have left the country. They didn't teach our people how to do the things we needed to do!"

(Later, after his ordeal was over, Pastor Silva would learn that the steam system had not broken down. The technique of almost starving prisoners in order to break their resistance was a carefully studied plan of action. This was orchestrated by larger world powers who had found it so successful.)

In their weakening condition the closely packed prisoners fought with one another constantly, throwing blows with the abandon that comes when hope is gone. Pastor Silva and his friends were constantly on their guard lest they be drawn into fights, some of which left the participants maimed and disfigured. The cell had become like a tinderbox, needing only a small flame to create emotional chaos.

Then one afternoon a shout went up from those who were clustered by the windows, "They're bringing a big boiler into the yard—it looks like the kind they use to cook food for the soldiers." And that was what it turned out to be. Wood was hauled into the prison yard, a fire was built under the boiler, and food was cooked. Eagerly the prisoners awaited the arrival of the guards to take them to their meal. Surely, at long last, they would have hot food.

As they entered the dining room, an overpowering stench filled their nostrils. With a sinking heart, Pastor Silva looked down at the unsavory mess which had been flung into dented aluminum bowls. It seemed to consist of small noodles cooked to a gluey paste with some sort of fish. But what kind?

"Does this fish have scales?" he asked his publishing secretary.

One of the prisoners at the table heard him and guffawed, "It certainly does. Don't you see the scales in front of you?"

And then Pastor Silva saw that the fish had been cooked scales and all with the noodles.

"Watch out for the worms!" another prisoner shouted. "They've cooked worms along with the noodles and fish."

The four of them tried to eat at least a few mouthfuls. But it was almost impossible to choke down the mess, in spite of their desperate hunger.

The next day the same "food" was served. And the next, and the next. Never a variation in the menu. No fruit or vegetables were ever given to the prisoners. The only variation was in the time at which they were fed. Sometimes it would be at noon, sometimes at two, sometimes at four, suiting the whims of the jailers.

Then the prisoners began to suffer violent gastro-intestinal sickness because obviously the fish was not fresh. With only one hole in the floor to care for physical needs, the situation in the cell deteriorated so horribly that Pastor Silva became convinced that the purpose of the jailers was to reduce them all to gibbering, mindless creatures who would never again think or act as men.

"I am not going to eat any more of that fish," he told his companions. "It is rotten. I cannot swallow it."

He went to one of the guards. "I have a request to make," he stated firmly. "I cannot eat that fish. May I please have just one slice of bread instead of the fish and noodles?"

The guard looked at him impassively. "I will ask," he said.

After that, Pastor Silva was occasionally given a small piece of bread when the others were served the fish stew. But just as often he was given nothing, so that his entire menu for the day was only a half slice of bread.

Now he began to suffer from lightheadedness, a side effect of starvation. Without his confiscated belt he could hardly hold up his trousers. His weight seemed to be going down a pound a day, as nearly as he could estimate.

One day he took a terrible risk. He was so desperate with hunger that nothing else seemed to matter. As he walked from the "dining room" where he had been given no bread, he saw the prison commander sitting not far away in the prison hall. Pastor Silva well knew that prisoners were forbidden to get out of line or to speak in the corridor, but he forgot all that in his great need.

Quickly he left the line and approached the prison commander.

"Sir," he said, "I cannot eat the fish. I have asked for a small piece of bread each time as a substitute, but I did not receive it today, and there have been many other days when I was not given the bread. Will you not ask the guards to give me just one small piece?"

Suddenly Pastor Silva became aware of what he had done. He

realized that his three companions were watching him and that other prisoners were watching. Obviously they expected that he would be punished for having spoken to the commander.

Upon hearing the request, the latter stood up silently, spoke not a word, turned on his heels, and left. Pastor Silva was confused. Would he bring guards, chain him to the wall, and have him beaten? Would the commander himself bring the bread?

Just as he was realizing that he must fall in at the end of the line of prisoners and return to the cell, the commander returned and silently handed him an entire loaf of bread! Later on he would look back on that loaf as one of the most precious symbols he had received in prison of God's care for him.

Suddenly words came from his lips which he could not believe. "I thank you from the bottom of my heart, sir," he said, "but could I make just one more request? I have three companions in my cell who cannot eat much of the fish. Could I have a loaf of bread for them?"

As silently as before, the commander turned and walked away. He brought back another loaf.

In the cell, almost delirious with joy, the four men divided the two loaves with great care.

This incident came at a time when Pastor Silva most needed some reassurance that a higher power was indeed in charge of the universe. It seemed to him that God leaned down from heaven and said, "Be not afraid. In your neediest hour I will take care of you." In fact, the words were so clear that he felt he could hear God speaking them. Though he had needed the bread more than he had ever needed food in his life, he needed even more the reassurance that the experience gave him. The action of the prison commander was so out of character, so unexpected, that it could not have been caused by anything less than God's power. On that the four companions were completely agreed. What prayers of thanksgiving they offered to God as they ate the bread—plain, a dish fit for a king!

Elena came every visiting day with clean underwear. She was strictly forbidden to bring any food. But through the prison bars she glimpsed his haggard face and saw how his shirt hung off his shoulders. She determined that she would find a way to get something edible to him. With loving care she always ironed and folded the few clothes that she was allowed to bring. One day an idea came to her as she and Maria and Lucila were eating lunch. (It was hard for them to enjoy any food, knowing of his cruel plight.) On this day they had soup and, with it, very thin little crackers.

"Girls," Elena said, "do you think it would be possible to conceal just a few of these crackers in Daddy's clean clothes?"

"Mother, the guards always inspect the clothes carefully," Maria answered fearfully.

"But they're used to you by now, and they know you won't be smuggling knives or anything like that," Lucila added.

Elena sat and pondered. If she tried to conceal the crackers and the guards discovered her plot, would this mean punishment for Antonio? Would it mean that never again would she be allowed to go into the prison yard to bring clean clothes and catch a glimpse of him?

She went into her bedroom and knelt, pouring our her problem to God. As she arose to her feet, she felt convinced she should try. "He looks as though he will starve to death before my eyes," she said to herself. "No matter what, I must try to get food to him."

Very carefully she concealed four of the wafer-thin crackers in the pocket of the shirt she was bringing him. When the guard took the clothes for inspection, she thought that her secret must be mirrored on her face, but somehow he did the most cursory inspection he had ever done. God was working. The crackers went in with the clean clothes.

Later, when they were reunited, Antonio had said to her, "I wept for joy when I found those four small crackers in my clothes. I was so very hungry. But the most wonderful part wasn't that they were food, but that they said 'I love you' to me, just as though I could hear your voice."

But though the crackers were responsible for great joy in Antonio's heart, they were also responsible for anxiety. He had to find places in his clothing to conceal the crackers. Realizing that Elena hoped to bring four more at her next visit, he would eat one small cracker each day. All went well. The crackers seemed like manna. On the day of her next visit, however, in the flurry of getting his dirty clothes to the guard when his name was called, he left his last little cracker in the pocket of his shirt.

"I could have wept for that tiny cracker," he later would tell Elena. "I can't even describe how sad I felt to lose that tiny bit of food."

Illness was ever present in the packed cell. The bodies of the prisoners quickly became so weakened by malnutrition and lack of good, sound sleep that they could not withstand germs. Pastor Silva longed for fruit and vegetables with such intensity that he could hardly put the thought of such things out of his mind.

Then he became very ill with such a sore throat that swallowing was agonizing.

"My throat feels as though two large stones are caught there," he told his companions. "I suppose I'm having an attack of tonsillitis." He was feverish, chilly, and totally miserable. Yet no medical attention was given to him. Each time he saw the guards when the prisoners were herded to meals, he begged to be taken to a physician. The guards listened impassively to his pleas but did nothing. With his towel he tried to prepare a compress for his throat to draw out the infection. But he had no hot water. He had nothing with which to treat himself. He was steadily becoming weaker.

When he had endured the condition for almost three weeks, to his surprise a guard opened the door and shouted, "Antonio Silva!" and gestured for him to follow. Dazed, he stumbled to his feet and followed the guard through the corridor, down the steps, and into the beautiful, blessed sunlight and fresh air. He was put in a car with a driver and two policemen, a man and a woman. They were very jolly with one another, totally ignoring him, even when they stopped at a snack bar for refreshments while he was kept in the car. His mouth watered, and his stomach convulsed as he saw the good food they were eating.

He knew that one of the laws of the new government was that no one could be given any medication unless the patient were admitted to a hospital. To give even a pill otherwise was punishable by imprisonment. What would happen next? His head was spinning with fever and wonder.

The hospital swarmed with what seemed hundreds—even thousands—of sick people and their relatives. "Come along," his guard commanded, pushing him rudely.

When the physician to whom he was taken examined his throat, he announced gruffly, "I don't see any trouble here."

Pastor Silva quietly replied, "I asked for the services of a doctor three weeks ago. I have done my best in the cell to take care of my problem. Perhaps it has turned the corner and is getting better. But I have another problem. My digestive system seems locked. My bowels have worked only four times in twenty-eight days. I know this is due to my diet, but can you help me?"

Silently the doctor handed him some pills. Then briefly he gave directions for taking them.

Out in the hall again, on impulse, Pastor Silva turned to the guard.

"Could you—would you—be so kind as to let me phone my wife?" he pleaded. "I am completely trustworthy. I will not try to run away."

The guard hesitated. Pastor Silva prayed silently. Then the guard blustered, "Make it brief!" But real sympathy showed in his eyes.

Pastor Silva rushed to a public phone, his heart pounding. His house, though only four blocks from the hospital, might as well have been on another planet. To his anguish, the first phone was not in working condition. Frantically he ran through the crowded hospital, searching for another. He completely lost the guard in the crowd. The thought occurred to him that it would be very easy to make his escape. But he had assured the guard that he could be trusted. Finally he found a working phone. Suppose no one was home! Would this precious, marvelous, surprising opportunity be wasted?

His heart in his mouth, he listened to one ring. Two rings. Three rings. "Oh, answer, please answer," he begged silently.

Then he heard the voice of Maria.

"Darling, call your mother, quick, quick!" he directed her.

"But Mother isn't here!" the little girl cried, bursting into tears at the shock of hearing her father's voice and her sorrow at her mother's absence.

"Don't cry, little one," he begged. "Where is Mother?"

"She's just down the street."

"Then run and tell her to come here to the hospital as fast as she can and tell her to bring me some fruit and some vegetables," he directed the child, sick at heart over Elena's absence. He could only hope and pray that little Maria had grasped what he had told her.

After assuring the child again of his love, he hung up the phone, frustrated, not daring to hope that the message would get to Elena in time. How merciless fate had been, he thought, sick at heart, to send her out of the house at just that moment. He slowly wove his way through the crowds of people, hoping to prolong the time so that Elena could get to the hospital. Finally he reached the side of the guard, who had apparently trusted him so completely that he showed no concern over his extended absence.

After a few more formalities were cared for and, papers signed, the other policeman from the car put in an appearance.

"It's time to go back to the prison," he ordered roughly. "Follow me into the car immediately."

Pastor Silva felt that he would almost rather die than give up this brief taste of freedom. He had been in the real world again; he had been rubbing elbows with people who were in charge of their own lives. He had been able to use a telephone like a normal person. He had talked with a doctor, man to man. How could he be taken back to the nightmare of the packed cell?

Moreover, could circumstances be so cruel as to deny him a glimpse of Elena, and possibly a word with her, face to face? Throwing caution to the winds, he begged humbly of the policeman driving the car, "My home is only a few blocks away. It would mean so much to me if only we could drive by it. Would that be possible?"

"Tell me the address," the man replied, noncommittally, promising nothing. But he turned the car at a corner which Pastor Silva realized would lead them past the mission building. His heart beat so heavily that he could see his shirt move. His mouth became dry. His tongue stuck to the roof of his mouth. He knew that he would not be allowed to go inside the house. Was there a chance that—?

Just then his eyes, straining to see as far as possible, identified two people running down the street. It was! It was Elena and Maria!

As the car approached them, he pleaded with the policemen.

"Oh, please, please—there are my wife and daughter. Please— won't you stop and let me have just a word with them?"

As a free man and a professional executive, he had never thought that he would be brought so low as to plead humbly with uneducated, toughened, and debased men for something that was his right. But he was past caring about human pride. He knew only that he must have a few moments with the two on the sidewalk.

Silently the driver pulled to the curb and stopped. Antonio leaped out with one great bound and clasped Elena in his arms.

"Oh, my darling," he said to her. "I thought that I would not be able to see you."

With muffled half-words and exclamations they attempted to communicate what was in their hearts, knowing that at any moment the guard would order Antonio back into the car.

"Are you all right, dearest?" Elena asked him anxiously. "Why were you at the hospital?"

"It's nothing," he told her. Just then Maria, who had not been able to run as fast as Elena, caught up with them and he gathered her also into his arms. Out of the corner of his eye he could sense the policemen in the car were becoming restless.

"Antonio," Elena whispered, "here are some cucumbers, some tomatoes, and some bananas. That's all I had in the house."

How beautiful the fruit looked! Surely this was not what the average person ate every day of his life, giving it not a thought! How could they not realize their good fortune?

"Into the car! Into the car!" the policeman at the wheel shouted.

Elena's arms tightened around him. He had to tear himself loose. For the sake of his wife and child he must not anger the guards. The three of them could not keep back the tears, however, as he slowly climbed back into the car. The motor roared. Soon the two on the sidewalk were only specks. He waved to them from the back window as long as he could see any sign of them.

The suddenness of the episode and the enormous flow of emotion had left him drained and disoriented. Then a dreadful thought struck him. Why, I am filthy and unkempt, with long, dirty hair and beard, and such grimy, uncut fingernails! I could even be carrying some terrible disease. Some of the prisoners look as though they are in the first stages of leprosy. What if I already have it and now I have exposed Elena and Maria by touching and kissing them? The joy of seeing them was almost overshadowed by fear and remorse.

Back in his cell he tried to grasp what had happened. In fact, he wondered if it had really happened or if it had been a dream manufactured from his great anguish and his overwhelming need. But the cucumber in his hand was real, with its smooth, satiny skin. And the taste! Surely no royal banquet was ever so tasty.

Then he pondered the conduct of the policemen. Certainly it had been out of character. It was almost unheard of to take a prisoner to the hospital unless he could no longer sit or stand. But he had been taken. And he had also been allowed the brief moment with his loved ones.

Later, in freedom, he would learn that one of the vice-presidents of the General Conference in Washington, D.C. (and a fellow Brazilian), had phoned Elena from the United States several days before to offer words of encouragement. He asked if she had information as to Antonio's physical condition.

"Word has reached us here in the United States that Pastor Silva is ill," he had told her.

Elena had been in anguish. "He has not sent word of this to me," she had replied. The hospital visit, coming so precipitously, and his haggard appearance struck deeper fear into her heart.

Later, a free man, Antonio would learn that obviously the telephone in his apartment was "bugged." The overseas call had been recorded and reported to designated government officials. Thus, after the three weeks when he had begged for medical attention to no avail, suddenly Pastor Silva had been hustled to the hospital, enabling the local government to claim that their treatment of him—and all other prisoners—was exceptionally humane. Probably this also accounted for the policeman's allowing him to greet Elena and to receive the food, Antonio later concluded.

A Miracle

Morale in the prison cell had become so low that threats of suicide among the prisoners were a daily occurrence. Only the four Adventist men, the Jehovah's Witnesses, and several other religious men had any hope to cling to. The majority of prisoners felt that they were pawns in a giant and mindless game, that they had been reduced to nonpersons. The prospects for the future were so bleak the daily struggle seemed not worth the effort.

When men of every class are packed together in such close confinement and denied normal satisfaction for their physical needs, homosexuality is almost certain to appear. Pastor Silva and the other Adventists hardly dared even give voice to their fears on this subject. Would they be assaulted? How would they protect themselves in case of attack? They prayed over and over for God's special protection. Their prayers were answered.

They began to notice that in a certain corner of the room near the toilet facility nearly every night furious fighting broke out, often just before dawn. Close as they were, they could not help observing that the brutal fights were caused by homosexual encounters. But it seemed almost as though unseen angels had formed a barrier—as though flaming swords had formed a wall around the four helpless men of God. Not once in their prison experience was Pastor Silva approached by a homosexual, nor were the other three.

Moreover, the truth of the old adage, "Birds of a feather flock together," was proven in that unlikely place, the packed cell. As the weeks and months passed by, the prisoners who seemed to be of a higher class, who were sober, who were trustworthy, made their way to the nucleus provided by "God's Four." They endured together.

Every day more prisoners were shoved into the small cell. The overcrowded conditions which had at first seemed intolerable now seemed almost luxurious by comparison. During all the long days, when there was absolutely nothing to do but think, and think, and think—with tortured thoughts and tired minds—the prisoners were packed so tightly together that changing positions even in the daytime became increasingly more difficult. As for getting any rest during daylight hours, it was impossible. Survival had become the goal. During the long hours when he stood motionless, when his feet and legs swelled out of proportion, with accompanying intense discomfort, Pastor Silva was always in a mental attitude of prayer. His communication with God was his lifeline.

Each day his tired nerves strained for the sound of an opened cell door and for the shout, "Antonio Silva!"

But it never came.

One morning a new sound penetrated the continual babble of voices, the shouts, the curses, and the moans. The men at the windows shouted, "Many trucks are coming into the prison yard!"

What did this mean? Was it a good omen or evil? Pastor Silva noticed that the older prisoners had grown strangely quiet. Do they know something about this that they will not tell? he wondered.

That afternoon all the prisoners learned what the trucks meant. The cell doors clanged open. A list of names was called. Pastor Silva and his three friends were not called. They could not know then how fortunate they were until they learned later that the trucks had taken prisoners to "relocation camps" hundreds of miles away. Not only men were taken, but women and children from other cells in the huge prison. Later they learned that the prisoners were forced to construct, out of branches and leaves, their own shelter from the elements.

No attempt was made to keep families together. Wives were sent with children to one camp, and husbands to another, with no prospect that they would ever meet again. In the prison cell Pastor Silva and his companions had befriended a very fine man, clean and courteous, whose wife was a baptized Jehovah's Witness. His story was a sad one.

"When the police came to our house to arrest us," he told them, "they asked if we were members of the Jehovah's Witnesses. Since I was not baptized, I told them truthfully that I was not. However, my wife was a member, and when they found that out, they loaded all of us—my wife, our children, and me—into police cars and brought us to

102

this terrible place. I have not seen my wife and children since we were imprisoned.''

On the day of the trucks, the man fought his way to a window—only to see his wife and children being loaded into one of the trucks. He could not shout loudly enough to get their attention. He did not know their destination. The experience was so shattering that he screamed in despair, ''Let me kill myself! Why must I live? I do not wish to live in such a cruel world!''

Pastor Silva was by his side in an instant, assuring him of God's unfailing love. ''God can watch over your wife and children just as well where they are going. Some day you will be released from prison. You will find them again. Let us pray together.'' They prayed, oblivious to the other prisoners, some of whom became quiet out of respect.

After the prayer the tortured man lapsed into quiet sobbing. ''I will never see them again,'' he repeated in a broken whisper. ''My life is over.'' Pastor Silva quoted some beautiful words from the ninety-first Psalm to him. ''For He shall give his angels charge over thee, to keep thee in all thy ways.'' After a while his sobbing ceased, but his spirit never seemed to recover. But he was not the only prisoner who would gladly have exchanged the half-life they were living for complete oblivion. However, belts and ties, and all other ''dangerous'' objects, had long ago been taken from the prisoners. They were doomed, it seemed, to live on and on, in a kind of earthly Hades.

After that first day of the trucks, it became a regular occurrence. In the beginning Pastor Silva and his companions had hoped that the unbearable crowding of the cell would be eased, though their sympathy was strong for those who were taken. Yet as fast as some of the prisoners left, new ones were shoved in. Compounding this daily disaster was a freak happenstance caused by the most torrential rainy season that anyone could remember. Because all major highways were flooded, prisoners could not be transported to the camps, but more and more were still shoved into the cell!

Two months passed, and they were well into December. Pastor Silva began to think of all the joys experienced during Christmas seasons of the past. This beautiful time, so rich with the meaning of Christ's birth, was something he and his family had always looked forward to with full hearts—always the beautiful songs, special church services, good food, and many guests. In many ways the Christmas season was the high point of the year. Would he spend this wonderful spiritual season here in this reeking cell?

One day, out of the blue, a prisoner came to him. "Pastor," he said, "could you preach a sermon for us here in the cell? We need something to give us hope." He was followed by other prisoners echoing this request.

This surprised Pastor Silva. He and His companions had prayed many times each day. They had never hidden the fact that they were pastors. But they had not, under the circumstances of the cell, felt it wise to make a "pushy" effort to bring their faith to the others. The tensions in the cell were so great that discretion seemed the only possible course to insure survival. But now requests had come, and they must make a decision.

The four Adventists talked it over. Everything in their training told them that they could not fail to answer this kind of call. "But," the young national colporteur told them hesitantly, "I know that there are very rough men in this cell along with some good men. I don't know how the rough ones might act if you preach. They are sure to make fun of you, and they might even try to harm you."

Painfully aware as they were that this might, indeed, be the case, Pastor Silva decided that he would try to preach one sermon on the love of Christ. Throughout the cell word was passed that one of the pastors would give a sermon. The very novelty of the idea caused quiet to fall—an eerie quiet, in contrast to the continual noise that had prevailed for almost twenty-four hours a day.

As he stood with the tightly packed men around him, Pastor Silva experienced a moment of panic. He scrutinized the faces so near his own, faces scarred by brutal fights, faces with glazed, empty eyes, faces which told the story of depravity. Never had he preached under circumstances such as these. The experience of Paul and Silas went through his mind. If those two biblical characters could minister to the needs of fellow prisoners, perhaps he could also. He had given much thought to what he would say. To his mind came the familiar texts that he wished to use, in all their power and majesty.

His was a simple sermon that day, an invitation to these desperate men to place their lives in Christ's hands, to ask forgiveness if they had committed crimes. He urged them to cast themselves on Christ's promises. Some were deeply moved. Others, however, as soon as the sermon was over, began telling their most obscene stories in the loudest voices. Many of the men joined in the raucous laughter. They hurled taunts at God. But Pastor Silva was not willing to give up.

"Let's try another service in a few more days," he told his friends.

They did, with the same results. This time, though, the stories were more obscene, if possible, and the taunts and laughter more raucous. Pastor Silva began to feel that the holy truths and the beauty of Christ were being profaned. Much as he regretted it, he sadly told his companions that it seemed best to him that they discontinue the preaching services.

Perhaps this decision was wise, for one of the guards had told a prisoner that if the preaching didn't stop, he would take steps to see that Pastor Silva was severely punished.

This did not mean that the four Adventists gave up their witnessing, however. They were always willing to talk with the prisoners and to give as much spiritual help and encouragement as possible under the oppressing circumstances.

But their physical bodies were becoming more and more depleted. Pastor Silva had found that the exertion of preaching, of raising his voice, and trying to remember all the texts, had reduced him almost to the fainting stage. Because of their extreme hunger, they seemed at times to be floating in a kind of half-world of shadows, where nothing seemed real. Pastor Silva began to fear for his mind. "Please don't let me become a different person. Please let me do some good here, in spite of conditions. Please give me an extra measure of physical strength," he prayed over and over.

The Lord answered his prayer abundantly. At this point in his incarceration prisoners began coming to him and to the other three in a continual flow. A question which they asked over and over, despairingly, was this: "If there is a God, and you say there is, why does He permit this terrible injustice? I have done nothing bad. I have been separated from my family. Why does God permit it?"

Then Pastor Silva and the others would develop the glorious theme of good versus evil since the foundation of the world. "God is permitting all this sorrow and injustice because everyone must be allowed to realize what it means when Satan takes over the hearts of men. There are beings in other worlds who are looking on to observe whether God is right or whether Satan is right. If God intervened in every situation, human beings would never realize the awfulness of sin. And the same is true of a government which rules God out of existence. Another supernatural power takes over."

But even though he enunciated the words with sincere conviction, at times it was difficult for Pastor Silva—hungry, dirty, his hair and beard longer and shaggier, his self-esteem nearly gone—to fully absorb the message he gave to others. He prayed constantly that he would not lose his own grip on God.

The hardened criminal element in the cell looked on, muttered sneers and threats, but did nothing more than that. However, one of the most terrifying aspects of life in the cell was the fact that as the days and weeks and months stretched out, a number of prisoners did lose their grip on sanity and became violent. Uncontrollable, they rolled about on the floor, screaming and foaming at the mouth. They had to be restrained from attacking other prisoners.

The nationals, with their background of witchcraft, were terrified.

"These men are possessed by the devil," they told the Adventists fearfully. "What will happen?"

These occasions, frightening as they were, gave Pastor Silva another opportunity to contrast the sweetness and calm of life in Christ with the way the devil takes advantage of those who follow him.

As the third month passed, Pastor Silva's physical sufferings seemed almost less than his mental suffering, denied as he was any reading matter. From the moment he awakened, through the cell cleanup, through the travesty of breakfast (and sometimes no meal for the rest of the day), there was absolutely nothing to do. His brain became tired from thinking, thinking, thinking. He and his companions reviewed all the doctrines of the Adventist Church. They exchanged stories of their childhood and youth and college days. They talked of their children, tears coming to their eyes as they remembered all the sweet and poignant incidents. But these reminiscences, though they absorbed some of the endless hours, always brought them to such sadness that they could hardly bear it, realizing all they had lost.

Often Pastor Silva remembered the stories his parents had told him about his relatives in the Old Country who had been thrown into prison and of those who had died there. Was this the way it had been with them—these endless days, the gnawing physical hunger, the despair, the hoping when there was no hope, the waiting for a door to open, for their names that were not called? He wished that he had asked his parents more questions about these people whom he had never known. They had been made of stern stuff, to withstand their terrible persecution and still remain true to God. He resolved over and over again that he would be as true as they and that he would not dishonor God by letting his spirit be defeated no matter what his eventual fate. He did not worry during this period so much about himself; his thoughts were constantly with Elena and Maria and Lucila. Though they tried to look cheerful in the brief glimpses he got during the "visits," his loving heart told him the story they tried so hard to conceal.

At one point a near-miracle occurred. At least Pastor Silva thought at the time that the incident belonged in that category. As he thought of his situation, it seemed to him that he *must* get word to the General Conference, especially to a Brazilian vice-president. (At that time he did not know that this man was in communication with Elena.) He reasoned that the vice-president could work with the Brazilian government to help effect his release. He could also work through the world church headquarters in Washington, D.C. But how could he get a message out of the prison?

One day, to his astonishment, one of the black prisoners whispered to him, "Pastor, I have a little piece of a pencil." And he produced the pitiful object. A diamond could not have looked more precious.

"Could I use it for just one message?" begged Pastor Silva.

"Yes," the man replied, "I will permit you."

Thinking aloud, Pastor Silva asked, "But what will I use for paper?"

Glancing about to be sure they were not overherd, the black prisoner whispered again, "I have a few sheets of paper."

Astounded, Pastor Silva held his breath. Dare he ask for anything so precious? Then, taking his courage in his hands, he entreated, "May I have just one scrap, please, please?"

The other prisoner pondered. He made up his mind. "I will give you half a sheet," he agreed.

It turned out that the two or three sheets were printed material from a very old copy of the *Reader's Digest*. The pages were very small. But to Pastor Silva they were a lifeline, a link with the real world, the savior of his sanity. His benefactor carefully put the remainder of the small sheets back in a hiding place he had contrived in the wall.

Then Pastor Silva sat down to think. He could hardly comprehend the magnitude of this miracle. He had no doubt that it was, indeed, a miracle sent from God. Why otherwise would the prisoner have approached him, all unbidden? He must not lose this opportunity. It might never come again. But how could he manage? Even if he hid the tiny note in his dirty clothes, how could Elena get it out of the country and on its way to Brazil? And even the ploy of the dirty clothes posed

The first letter Antonio Silva wrote from prison was written to his division president headquartered in Berne, Switzerland. For stationery, a fellow prisoner offered this old page from a *Reader's Digest* magazine. Antonio wrote on both sides.

108

a risk, for while the guards did not examine the outgoing clothes as thoroughly as the incoming, they usually gave them a perfunctory shake. If I write my message and fold it into a very tiny shape, and place it deep in my dirty trouser pocket, and pray, pray, pray, he reasoned to himself, perhaps it will get through.

To the vice-president he wrote a brief message in the margins of the printed sheet. Then, to Elena, on the same sheet, he wrote, ''Mail this outside the country. Give it to the mother of the girl that comes to play with our daughters.''

With his heart in his mouth he gave his dirty clothes to the guards on Elena's next visit. Bored with the endless clothes routine, this time they did not examine the dirty clothes at all. Another miracle. Elena found the tiny note—again a miracle—for she wondered why she sensed such a strong impulse to feel inside the pockets, pockets which had always in the past been completely empty. Her heart almost beat out of her chest as she unrolled the tiny note. It was like hearing Antonio's loved voice! For one brief moment she could almost pretend that this was a note from him when he was on a trip and that he was coming home. But the awful reality washed over her again.

Immediately she understood his message. All mail in and out of the country was now subject to intense scrutiny, especially mail from and to foreigners. Mailing the note locally would be totally fruitless. But the husband of the woman whom Antonio mentioned was a truck driver who crossed the border into other countries routinely. He was known by the border guards and was not searched.

Her prayers and much of her heart went with the note when she gave it to the faithful woman. Her husband took it across the border with no trouble, bought the proper stamps, and put it in the mail himself. The vice-president received it; and, though he had been working tirelessly in Antonio's behalf, he redoubled his efforts. He even used the sad note as the basis for sermons, begging the believers in Brazil to pray every day for Pastor Silva's release. But Pastor Silva would not know this until months later. He could only wonder through the long days and nights if the note had reached its destination.

Seeing the tiny bit of printed matter had served to whet his appetite for mental food. He refused to give up the possibility that something might be slipped into the cell for him to read, once the note had been smuggled out. So on one of Elena's visits to him in the courtyard, he was able to make her understand—another miracle, at such a distance—that above all things (other than food) he wanted reading material. After he realized that she understood what he was saying, above the din of all the prisoners shouting at their relatives, he was sick with fear. If she tried to smuggle reading matter into the cell, would she also be imprisoned? Had he again jeopardized her life and the lives of the little girls?

But he had underestimated Elena—again. Inside the next batch of clean clothes, folded into the tiniest of squares, were several pages from denominational magazines. When he found them, he almost wept aloud! Invincible Elena! What a remarkable woman was this wife of his. Had he known all that she was doing while he was in prison, he would have had even more heart-stopping moments. But just the sight of printed pages was a joy so great as to overwhelm him. After he had read the pages over and over and over, he shared them with his three friends. When they had finished, the prisoners in the cell who were literate begged for a chance. Everyone had his turn. The pages were handled as though they were the most precious objects in the world.

"You know," Pastor Silva said to his publishing secretary one day, "wouldn't it be wonderful if we had a camera in here and could take some pictures of these condemned prisoners avidly reading our denominational pages? It certainly would give our publishing brethren a big thrill!"

Then both men threw back their heads and laughed. It was the first time they had laughed since their imprisonment! The ludicrousness of their situation struck them—a camera, there in prison, showing the effectiveness of Adventist literature!

Now a ray of light pierced the darkness, for if Elena could, at times, smuggle a few sheets of printed matter to him, surely he could devise a way to send an occasional message to her. Oh, the comfort and joy if he could just communicate a few words of love. But his hopes seemed dashed on visiting day, when Elena had tried to convey a message to him. She had been successful with the first few sheets, but on this particular day when the guards shook the clothes vigorously, the little sheet with her writing on it fell out. Angrily, with a shout, the guard threw the clothes in all directions. Watching from the window, Pastor Silva nearly wept as he saw Elena's stricken face. He received no clean clothes that day.

He determined to watch the method the guards used in examining the clothes. The pockets of the shirts were searched, but the one towel which the prisoners were allowed was merely shaken out in a desultory manner.

"Ah," he said to himself, "if Elena would sew a larger hem into the towel, then she could roll up a tiny piece of paper, and I don't think it would be detected."

But how could he make her understand?

On the next visiting day, when it was his turn at the window, he shouted at her, "Elena, use a towel! Use the towel!"

For a moment she stared at him, puzzled. Then a great light broke over her face, and she nodded emphatically. "I will, Antonio, I will!"

Still he could not be sure that she had understood. The days between the visits were filled with tension. Again, he suffered deep fear and regret. Had this move been fatally unwise?

When Elena came to the prison yard the next time with his clothes, his heart was in his mouth. Peering from the window, he watched the guards examine the shirt pocket and shake out the towel. They motioned to the other guard to take the clothes to Antonio and receive his dirty clothes.

Pastor Silva took his clean clothes from the guard with a completely impassive face. He waited until he was sure that no one in the packed cell was watching him. Then, very carefully, he unfolded the towel, felt along the seam—and there it was! Elena had taken her sewing machine, put another hem in the towel, a larger hem than the towel had originally had, and into that tubular space she had placed tiny bits of paper filled with messages. Pastor Silva's problem, though, was how to get the hem open. He had no scissors, no knives, no sharp objects. But he did have long fingernails. In fact, one of the most distressing features of his imprisonment and that of his friends was that they had absolutely no way to groom themselves. Their nails had grown so long that the men felt as though they were kin to Nebuchadnezzar in the book of Daniel. Their only recourse was to rub their nails up and down the cinder-block walls.

For once Antonio was glad for his long, ragged nails. He was able to pick open the seam and find the precious bits of paper. Such deep emotion shook him at the sight of Elena's handwriting that he had to crouch on the floor for a few moments. No beautiful letter that she would write him in future years could ever mean as much as those few messages of love scribbled on scraps of paper.

"I must get a message back to her," he said to himself. "Shall I use the same method?" Although the guards were haphazard in their

11/4/76

Meu querida Lélia

Que Deus mantenha você continuamente sob seus cuidados!

Faz duas semanas que não lhe escrevo e que também nada recebo de você. É que no dia 1 de Abril, justo quando completava 160 dias de prisão, lá onde você ia me visitar, fui transferido para a prisão em frente ao Pio XII, onde você estudou temporariamente. Aqui é bem melhor. Há espaço para dormir (no chão), para andar, e há um campo de futebol no fundo, com árvores em volta, que permite tomar sol, fazer exercício, etc. Aqui mamãe pode trazer-me comida todos os dias, só que as visitas são mais raras. Assim, nada tenho sabido de você nestes últimos 15 dias. Quando mamãe traz comida, só a posso ver um

A reproduction of an actual letter that Antonio Silva sent to his wife from prison. Letters such as these were folded many times and hidden in dirty socks.

examination of outgoing dirty clothes, still he did not wish to jeopardize either Elena's safety or the delicate communication line they now had going. His still-facile brain began to work at full speed. What one object of clothing would the guards not like to handle? Of course! Dirty socks! He would scribble a few lines on one of the papers and bury it deep in his dirty socks.

On the next visit, when his turn at the window came, he shouted to Elena, trusting that the general noise would cover his words, "The socks! The socks!"

She nodded, signaling that she had grasped his meaning. And so it was! The guards seemed totally uninterested in exploring the socks of the prisoners. Thus a saving lifeline of communication was set up between Antonio and Elena, a lifeline that was further strengthened when she managed to conceal the refill for a ballpoint pen in his clean clothes. Riches inexpressible! Now he no longer had to beg the prisoner for the pencil stub.

Throughout his imprisonment, the lice in the cell were a severe trial to Pastor Silva. He wondered if he were especially susceptible to their bites, or if his body in some way possessed an unusual attraction for them. Bitten day and night, his body became a mass of small sores. He felt that if his clothes could be dusted with some kind of insect powder, or disinfectant, he might get relief. With the line of communication between him and Elena now working, she got his message and used the disinfectant on all his clean clothes. Finally his body began to recover from infected bites.

He wasn't the only one so afflicted. Some of the prisoners had taken to wearing their clothing inside out, reasoning that the lice hid in the seams and borders. Other prisoners, when they could obtain soap, smeared it over their bodies. This accomplished its purpose, but the irritation proved as uncomfortable as the louse bites.

As the weeks and months crawled by, Antonio's lengthening beard and hair, matted and filthy, caused him much discomfort. But try as he and the others might, they could devise no way to cut their hair and beards. They looked at one another, wondering if their friends would recognize them if they were to pass on the street.

One day, though, this changed. One of the prisoners, it was rumored, had received from his family a razor blade imbedded in a bar of soap. Of course this was not an unmixed blessing—a razor blade could be used as a weapon. With the tension in the packed cell ever rising, that razor blade in the wrong hands meant murder.

But the urge to groom himself, even slightly, was too great for Pastor Silva to resist. Approaching the prisoner with the rusty razor blade, Pastor Silva asked politely, "Would you let me use your blade to cut my beard? It causes me much discomfort."

Readily the prisoner agreed.

The shave with the rusty blade was a fantastic luxury. How light and free Antonio felt with all that hot, matted beard off his face! How much more hopeful life seemed! Somehow he felt more like himself than he had felt in months. But would the guards not notice his changed appearance? That thought pierced him like a knife. He had not realized that this might happen. An icy finger ran down his spine. He tried to keep his face turned away whenever the guard opened the door. To his relief nothing was said.

The problem with food was now becoming intense. The energies of the four friends seemed almost depleted. They saw themselves in the first stages of malnutrition, knowing this condition could affect their thinking and their judgment. Earnestly they engaged in seasons of prayer, beseeching God to give them food, but if this were not to be, to bestow upon them extra measures of strength and energy in spite of their condition.

The turning point came, and thus the answer to their prayers, in a totally unexpected way. Pastor Silva believed then, and will believe until he dies, that the answer was a direct miracle from God. One Sabbath morning he and his friends had had their pitiful "Sabbath School," which had been their custom. They each recited favorite Bible verses, discussed them, had prayer, and asked God for a special Sabbath blessing in the cell.

In many ways Sabbath was the worst day of the week. Then their thoughts were continually on their families, Sabbath School, the preaching service, the warm fellowship of other believers, and all the things which had made life dear. Pastor Silva finally found a small spot near a window where he could look out at the blue sky and white clouds. He saw an occasional bird flying wild and free. Every nerve and muscle cried out to join it. If only he had wings and could lift himself out of his malignant cell.

Then he noticed a frail-looking young man, whom he estimated to be in his early twenties, standing beside him, despair all over his face. They fell into conversation.

"I have been very sick," the young man told him.

During the months of imprisonment some of the prisoners would from time to time become seriously ill. Malnutrition, lack of exercise, lack of cleanliness took their toll. But it was impossible to get attention from the guards. So the prisoners themselves had devised a system. When it was apparent that one of their number was critically ill, they would set up such a noise and commotion that the guards would be forced to open the door to investigate. Quick as a wink, having planned their strategy carefully, they would place the body of the sick man in the door so that it was impossible for the guards to close the cell again. Then they would pack themselves tightly behind the sick body, making it impossible to shove it back into the room. That any sick man survived such brutal measures was surprising, but the young man had done just that.

"When the guards were forced to take me to a hospital, I was given treatment and decent food," he said. "When I got better, the doctor gave me a prescription saying that I must be allowed to have certain kinds of food." At this time in the city most good foods were unavailable unless ordered by a doctor or secured by a family member who would stand in lines, hours at a time.

When they brought me back here, I expected them to take away my food slip. But I guess they didn't examine my clothes very carefully, because I still have it," he concluded.

Although Pastor Silva had been listening politely, he did not really understand that he was in the beginning of a miracle.

"You see," the young man went on, "I've heard that if the prison commander will sign this doctor's slip, then my family could bring food to me."

"Well," Pastor Silva exclaimed in amazement, "why haven't you tried to get him to sign it?"

The young man sighed, "My mother is very poor. She would not have the money to buy food or the strength to stand in line. I'm afraid she would bring me her own little store of food, and she would starve. She is a widow and really has nothing."

Quick as a wink, Pastor Silva's brain flashed a signal.

"Let me tell you how I think I can help you and myself and my friends," he exclaimed in a forcible whisper. "Give me the doctor's prescription. I think I can smuggle it out to my wife with a message. She will have it signed by the commander; then she will bring food to you which you will share with me and my three friends."

The young man seemed dazed. "Do you think you can do this?" he whispered fearfully.

"Yes, I can. My God is all powerful. He will work for us," replied Pastor Silva, somehow confident that the plan would work.

In the next batch of dirty clothes, he concealed the doctor's precious slip—the most important piece of paper yet to be in his hands. He concealed another small note explaining the plan to Elena.

It seemed to him that he would snap from the tension on the day those particular dirty clothes were sent out. He had had no trouble with the "dirty sock plan" until now. Would the devil influence the guards to make an unusual search?

The Lord prevailed. Elena got the message.

Later Pastor Silva would learn that Elena had inquired desperately of the others who were in the mission (the publishing secretary's wife and family had moved in with her for security reasons), and finally she was told that a certain woman in the church might get the prescription signed by the prison commander. Without telling her any of the details and with her heart in her mouth, Elena asked the church member to try to get the signature.

How she and the others prayed! Of course Pastor Silva knew nothing of all this as he and his companions did their own praying in the cell. They would not know until months later what had happened outside the prison walls.

They waited fearfully for Monday to come. They took turns looking out the window whenever they could get near enough to do so. Would they receive some food? Would the young man's name be called to come to the door? The suspense was unbearable.

"Look!" Pastor Silva almost shouted. Coming into the prison courtyard was the son of the publishing secretary, accompanied by a policeman. He was carrying a large bag of food. The young man who had implemented this miracle made his way toward the door, suddenly courageous. The four held their breath. Would something even yet go wrong?

In a few moments a guard opened the door, shouted the young man's name, gave him the bag, and quickly clanged the door shut. Faithfully the young man brought the bag to the corner where the four men were standing, motionless. When they opened the bag and viewed its contents, they actually wept with joy and gratitude. Would any future delight be as marvelous as this?

Pastor Silva and his friends would live to eat many delicious meals, but nothing would ever taste or look so good as this; no food ever again would contain the assurance of love and sanity, and the reassurance that, come what may, God would provide. Roasted potatoes (so tasty!) and thick, luscious sandwiches, with extra lettuce (which Pastor Silva could hardly eat because it looked so green and beautiful) were never more delicious!

The menu on the second day was even more sumptuous: sandwiches, a plastic container filled with boiled rice and boiled eggs, and an orange for each man, a tomato for each, and—luxury beyond belief—cashew nuts! At first they wondered how they would eat the rice with their dirty hands, but they need not have worried. The stalwart wives had hidden plastic spoons at the bottom of the bag.

"We are eating like human beings again," Pastor Silva told the delighted men, after they had bowed their heads and offered the most fervent thanks of their lives.

For Elena and the publishing secretary's wife, and also church members, finding food for the daily visit took up the major share of their time, Pastor Silva would later learn. The faithful "suppliers" would stand in line for hours at the markets to find beans, corn, cucumbers, crackers, and whatever else they could afford.

Pastor Silva found it especially touching that when oranges were included in the food sacks, Elena and the others would have peeled off the outer part of the orange skin. Given the fact that the men had only their long, dirty fingernails with which to peel, this thoughtfulness indicated a high degree of perceptive caring.

Much later, Pastor Silva would learn that the first food on the beginning "food day" was prepared by the wife of another pastor. When the permission to bring the food arrived, very little time remained before the visiting period. There was no time to search out a market for supplies, but she gave the food from her kitchen.

The daily miracle continued, with only a few exceptions, for the remainder of the time that Pastor Silva and his companions were in that packed cell. As the four of them contemplated it with never-ending wonder, and as their strength and optimism began to return—the result of better nutrition—they thanked the Lord over and over. The frail young man prayed along with them, though he had previously known nothing of God.

Actually, some of the other prisoners had been recieving food from the outside in a kind of "black market" arrangement. Pastor Silva had been aware of a good deal of bribing of guards and of smuggled food during the night. But he also had learned, by discreet inquiries, that the amount of money the guards insisted on receiving from families was incredibly high. Even so, the families had no assurance that the food would be given to their loved ones. He had felt, in spite of their desperate need, that he and his companions could not get involved in this. If the bribery were discovered, it could lead to their being kept in prison for the remainder of their lives. But with the legitimate "prescription" they were safe.

"Thou preparest a table before me in the presence of mine enemies," were the words that sprang to his mind every day when the food came.

Later, when he was free again, he would learn that the bringing in of the food had not been nearly as smooth a process as he had thought from his position inside the cell. In fact most of the time it was a chilling and threatening experience for the devoted ones on the outside. When Elena and the others would bring the food to the prison yard, over and over the guards would shout at them, "This is the last time you can bring food! Don't come here again! Do you hear? This is the last time!"

The women would bow their heads meekly—and show up the next day as usual as though nothing had happened.

He would also learn that when his publishing secretary's son was sent back to Brazil for safety's sake, Elena and the publishing secretary's wife became the regular conveyors of the food. To enter the prison yard with the rough soldiers, and with relatives of some of the prisoners who were hardened criminals, and to be stared at insolently, knowing that they had no one on which to call for help if they were attacked, was a never-ending terror. Antonio would learn also that when the two women would arise early each morning to go to the market with their slender resources to purchase food, they would feel their nerves beginning to tighten. Then home again they worked in almost total silence, the tension so great that they were unable even to talk with one another. Would their dear husbands get the food this day? Would the two of them also be thrown into prison for disobeying the guards' orders to cease bringing food?

At the same time other problems in the cell were increasing.

The total frustration of keeping between 150 to 200 men locked together in such a small area with no activity and no real place to sleep brought tempers at times past the boiling point and to inevitable explosions. On one particularly hot, humid, and endless afternoon, fight after fight broke out in the cell. Blood poured from the wounds inflicted by fists, teeth, and fingernails. Curses filled the air.

118

"We must stay here by the wall and be as quiet as possible," Pastor Silva whispered to his companions, knowing that the temper of the other prisoners could easily turn against him and the publishing secretary, because of their white skin. The riot boiled to a crescendo, until one of the guards was forced to open the door to investigate.

"FREEDOM! FREEDOM!" the prisoners screamed as the doors opened, and in a great tidal wave they broke through the door and out into the hall, carrying Pastor Silva and the others along with them like flotsam and jetsam in a boiling flood.

"Don't try to turn back!" Pastor Silva shouted to his friends. "The others might kill us, or we might be trampled to death!"

The swirling, shouting, cursing mob spilled out into the yard, some of them stopping to force open the doors of other prison cells. Out of these cells poured scores of prisoners as frustrated, angry, and desperate as the others. In about three minutes more than 1000 prisoners were milling about in the prison yard, shouting defiance and rage.

"Pray, brethren!" was Pastor Silva's admonition. Prayer was the only weapon they had. Would they lose their lives in this riot? Never had death seemed closer.

Amid the wild shouts, screams, upraised fists, and gestures of defiance, the prison commander organized his guards. They formed a tight circle around the prisoners with lowered shotguns and rifles. The guards, though, were so outnumbered by the prisoners that Pastor Silva wondered how they could establish control. His blood turned to ice when the ringleaders began a chant quickly taken up by most of the 1000 men:

"Seize the guards' guns! Seize the guns! Seize the guns!"

No one, however, was willing to be the first to risk certain death.

All realized that the guards would shoot a few of the men while the others were taking over. So there was a momentary stalemate.

Then, to the relief of the four companions, soldiers began to pour over the walls on all four sides of the prison block. They carried not only guns, but large whips and clubs. When the rioting prisoners saw what was happening they screamed in terror, "RUN! RUN!"

But there was no place to run. The clubs and whips came down on sculls and flesh with sickening thuds and with no mercy. The screams of those being beaten mingled with the screams of those trying to find a place to hide.

Pastor Silva and the other three seemed paralyzed. Although they had no part in the rebellion, the soldiers would not know this; besides it would probably have made no difference.

Suddenly Pastor Silva felt a searing pain across his back. He too was being beaten. He twisted and turned, trying to escape his tormentor. Out of the corner of his eye he saw that his three friends also were being beaten unmercifully. Had there not been so many prisoners to discipline, their fate might have been sealed right there in the prison yard, he later thought. But he and his friends were not seriously injured. After comparing bruises and lesions when the guards had finally quieted the rebellion and had herded the prisoners into their cells, the four said to each other in profound gratitude, "Let us thank God for preserving our lives through this terrible riot."

This hard experience, though, was not as frightening as one that occurred a short while later. Throughout the day the men packed in the cell had been unbearably restless. They had screamed their hatred of the injustice of being put into prison with no trial, with no formal accusations, and with no information as to when, if ever, they would be released.

"We don't have to endure this foul treatment! They call this justice—well, let's show them some justice of our own!" one of the more violent prisoners grated in a voice which could be heard throughout the cell. The guards on the outside, however, gave no evidence of having heard him.

"How could we show any JUSTICE?" mocked others.

Then he told them his plan. "Tomorrow, if the guard opens the door for any purpose—not for breakfast, for he has other guards with him then—but if he opens it during the day, we'll seize him and drag him inside. We'll show him what JUSTICE means!" he concluded, drawing his hand across his throat.

Fired by the determination of this man, the others shouted agreement. They also made the motion of cutting the throat.

Pastor Silva listened, horror-stricken. It was impossible to tell whether they actually meant to murder the guard, but he feared this was the case. If this crime took place, all the prisoners in the cell would be held equally accountable. In effect, they would all then be classed as murderers. This would mean the death sentence for every man in the cell. After all that he and his companions had endured, would they end their lives before a firing squad in this remote corner of Africa? Would they have to surrender their lives so senselessly?

Then another more terrifying thought struck both him and the publishing secretary simultaneously. If the day went as usual, the seventeen-year-old son might be bringing food to them. By this time the routine seemed to have been established so that the teenager went alone to the prison commander's office to report that he was bringing the "prescribed" food; then a soldier came to the door of the cell, opened it, and the food was given. (Some time later, Elena and the other women had taken over the food routine.)

Pale with apprehension, Pastor Silva and his publishing secretary talked over this development.

"If they carry out their threat, then your son could easily be caught in the middle and might possibly lose his life," Pastor Silva whispered.

His friend was almost in tears. "Isn't there some way we can send a warning?" he implored.

But try as they might, they could think of no way. How earnestly they sought the Lord during the long night hours! They pleaded over and over that He would intervene and do what they were powerless to do.

Finally the night merged into dawn. Then the cell-cleaning routine. Then breakfast. Then the waiting, waiting, waiting.

At the window where he had stationed himself, the publishing secretary saw his young son enter the courtyard.

"He's here!" he whispered to the others.

Instantly the four of them began a season of silent prayer. They were still praying, their eyes closed, when they heard the guard begin the process of unlocking and opening the massive door.

During these hours the prisoners had been inflaming one another's hatreds and resentments to flash point. Being familiar now with the food routine of the four, the prisoners knew that the soldier would soon open the door if all went as usual.

"Now remember," urged the ringleader, "the minute the door is fully open, grap the guard and drag him inside—"

The door opened, inch by inch. Nothing happened. The food was passed in. Still nothing happened. The guard closed and locked the cell.

Weak with relief, Pastor Silva and the others sent their fervent thanks up to God. They would never know why the planned attack had not taken place, but they would always feel, through all the days of their lives, that God had sent angels to the cell to restrain the prisoners.

Good-bye to the Little Girls

For the four companions, existence had become very much like walking a tightrope. They dared not antagonize the other prisoners, yet they could not enter into their vicious schemes and plans. Nor, in their desires not to anger the guards, did they wish the guards to favor them, thus bringing down on their heads the wrath of the other prisoners.

But the guards, as the weeks wore on, began to sense the difference in the lives and attitudes of the four. Often when the guards had to enter the cell—a task they would do only with cocked pistols—they spoke of this difference to the other prisoners.

"We always have to come in here to settle your quarrels," they told the most violent prisoners. "But we never have any trouble with the pastors. Why is that?"

Although happy that their lives were providing a positive witness for Christ in this setting, the four friends were not sure that it was best for the guards to hold up their conduct as an example.

As the months dragged on, Pastor Silva's physical condition improved. He tried desperately to maintain mental stability; though, at times, the apparent hopelessness threatened to overwhelm him. Fortunately, the four friends had learned to sense when one of their number was in dire need of spiritual help. Somehow on these occasions each was able to take his turn at encouraging the most downcast.

One Sabbath morning—after three long months—Pastor Silva realized that it was about nine o'clock. The long Sabbath must be lived through, the day which continued to be the most heartbreaking of the week. He was offering a silent petition asking for peace of spirit, when suddenly, as if in a dream, the cell door clanged open.

"Antonio Silva!" the guard roared. "Come with me!"

Struck dumb and almost paralyzed, Pastor Silva stood rooted to the spot. He had dreamed and hoped for just such a summons for so long. What could it mean? Was it really happening? Was there—could there be—a prospect of freedom at long last? He had no time to say anything to his companions, but his eloquent glance was enough. They would pray.

Quickly the soldier propelled him down the prison corridor, out the door, down the steps, and into a police car. Startled, shocked, unable to believe that he was in the outdoors after this long time, Pastor Silva tried to gaze in every direction at once, taking in every sight. If only Elena were walking by! If only he could have just a glimpse of her!

But it was not to be. In just a few minutes the police car pulled up to the Criminal Investigation Building, the place where his wretched imprisonment had begun.

With a sense of unreality, of déjà vu, Antonio Silva found himself taken to the very office of the grim-faced inspector. With a sense of greater unreality he saw the same inspector, at the same desk, with the same threatening expression on his face. It was as if three months had not occurred, and he had simply been sentenced to a limbo of bare existence, barely better than that of a despised dog.

Obviously, he thought, he would be interrogated again. Would he be tortured now? But before the inspector could begin, he was called out of the room. To watch Pastor Silva (whom he seemed to consider a dangerous criminal) the inspector sent a young guard. Pastor Silva estimated him to be about twenty years old. As the two sat in silence, the young man eyeing the pastor contemptuously, suddenly it flashed into Antonio's mind that when the apostle Paul was imprisoned, he always made it a point, if possible, to tell the story of his own conversion.

To himself Pastor Silva said, "I wonder if Paul did this for a special purpose. He must have thought that his story would awaken common chords in the lives of others. Besides he may have thought that he could accomplish more this way at times than by direct answers to interrogators." The more he thought of this, the more he resolved that he would try to tell the story of his own conversion to the young soldier. But how should he begin?

Suddenly the way opened, when the soldier broke the silence with a sneer.

"So you believe in God, do you?" he challenged.

Just as Pastor Silva was about to give the conventional and customary answer, his lips almost of their own volition seemed to shape another answer.

"Let me answer you this way," he replied courteously. "No nation can become strong if the people themselves will not be honest and good. This means that each citizen of a nation must have his own set of strong moral and ethical beliefs."

Pastor Silva could see that he had captured the young soldier's attention. Going on, he told the boy a story out of his past.

"When I was a boy of about twelve or thirteen, I began to learn some bad things. If I had continued in those habits, I would have been led into a very dark future. Things continued along that way until I was fifteen. I seemed to be torn by two different viewpoints, and I couldn't make up my mind what I wanted to think or how I wanted to live. But then, somehow there came into my heart a strong desire to study the Bible, the Word of God. I resolved that I would not go to bed without studying some part of the Bible."

Though the young soldier had said nothing, his eyes were riveted on Pastor Silva's face. He had begun to lean forward slightly.

"After I had spent some nights in Bible study, I felt an overpowering urge to pray. Something in me said that I must pray to the living God. I wanted to pray aloud and really feel that I was communicating with God. But I didn't want anyone else to hear me; so this is what I did: at night, after I had read the Bible, I used to go out in the backyard and there, beneath a tree, I would kneel down and open my heart to God. I told him all my plans. I asked His guidance in all my decisions. I asked Him to watch over every aspect of my life. After I had followed this practice for some time, I realized that things in my life were getting better and better. I had the power to overcome the temptations to evil that had been so much a part of my earlier life."

Pastor Silva could see that the young soldier was taking in every word. But what would be his reaction? Would he recommend to the police inspector that the pastor be kept in prison forever? Whatever the consequences, Pastor Silva felt that God wanted him to continue with his testimony.

"Later, as the years went on, I felt very strongly that God had a definite plan for my life."

Then Pastor Silva went through the story of the almost miraculous way that he had earned money to go to college, even when he was far past the age that most people would have considered proper to get a college education. He told the young man about his marriage, how he had taken God into his planning and confidence, and what a beautiful and loving home he and Elena shared.

"Now we have been married nearly seventeen years, with never a cross or ugly word between us. We live in an atmosphere of love—not because I am a good person, but because the power of God has transformed my heart, and it is my dearest pleasure to live as He wants me to live."

Pastor Silva stopped speaking. There was total silence in the office. In a final summation of belief, he stated softly to the young officer, "God has done so much for me; I could never stop believing in Him."

Suddenly anguish showed on the face of the young soldier. He wrung his hands together, stood to his feet, started toward the door, and these words were almost wrenched from his mouth: "I, I, too." He rushed from the room, locking the door from the outside. Pastor Silva then realized that this young soldier had been denying his belief and his conscience. He was a soul in torment. How thankful Pastor Silva was that he had given his testimony. As he sat there in the silence alone, he asked God to keep working on the heart of the young soldier and to give him no peace until he made his surrender.

The inspector returned. With total disinterest, he tossed a few questions at Pastor Silva. He seemed too bored even to listen to the answers. Nothing was accomplished.

His disappointment so great that he could hardly bear it, Pastor Silva was put in the car and driven back to prison. He had hoped so much, had felt that surely this time he would be free. When he entered the packed cell, the disappointment on the faces of his friends equaled his own. As he thought of the hours just spent, however, there was one ray of light. He had encountered a soul in need. He had not been given freedom, but he had been given an opportunity to witness.

As always, during the days following his disappointment, Elena and Maria and Lucila filled his thoughts. He knew that Elena would never send him a message which would make his lot in prison harder. He knew that she would never tell him of persecution and trials and fears she might be suffering. His mind twisted and turned during the long hours of the nights. He should be either protecting his wife and daughters in this strange and threatening land, or he should take them home—but he could do nothing. How were they being treated? Would the power of the gospel be sufficient to cause the national church members to love and protect them? Would they be in danger from those who had formerly been their friends, from believers as well as nonbelievers? Sometimes he felt that he would go mad with these thoughts, especially when some of the other prisoners received smuggled information about treatment of white women.

"White women are being raped when they show their faces on the streets," some of the prisoners taunted. Apparently they were happy at the thought of humiliation and brutality shown to those of another race.

His heart pounding, Pastor Silva sent silent prayers heavenward for protection for his three "girls." He could count on Elena's good judgment. He knew her to be very, very courageous. Yet, her courage and her determination to secure his release might place her in even greater danger. He and his companions shared these terrible thoughts with one another. Finally they came back to the only comfort they had, the only comfort that never failed—prayer and a feeling that God would watch over their dear ones, no matter what the circumstances.

Pastor Silva now had begun to think incessantly of what the future might hold for his wife and girls. He was not able to give them the protection they needed. During the long night hours he prayed to be shown how to advise Elena, who had always accepted his counsel as head of their home. Finally he became convinced that the three of them should return to Brazil. If God willed him to be released, this would be done. If not, he would live out what remained of his life in prison.

He began sending messages to Elena on the bits of paper. "You must take the girls and go back home to Brazil. It is not safe for you here, and you can do nothing more for me," he told her. But always, the answer would come back, with loving stubbornness, "I will never go and leave you, Antonio. Do not ask me to leave you."

Her love and devotion were his lifeline, next to God's presence. As he began to realize that no power on earth could cause her to leave him in this strange land, imprisoned, he changed the tenor of his messages. "Elena," he finally wrote, "if you will not go, then send our little daughters. We have loving relatives in Brazil who would care for them as their own." It cost him a great deal to suggest that his beloved little girls be sent so far across the ocean by themselves, without either father or mother.

"I will arrange to send them home, Antonio," was the message

4 DE FEVEREIRO DE 19[..]

MUI QUERIDA FILHA LÍVIA

PAPAI GOSTARIA MUITO DE VIAJAR DE SEU
LADO PARA O BRASIL. CREIO QUE LOGO ESTAREI
SOLTO, MAS O FUTURO É DESCONHECIDO. TENHO ESPERANÇAS
DE UM DIA AINDA MORAR[...] JUNTOS, MAS ESCREVO-LHE
PARA O RESTO DA VIDA.

EU GOSTO MUITO DE VOCÊ, E LEMBRO COM
SAUDADE QUANDO FICAVA OLHANDO DURANTE HORAS O BEBEZINHO NO
BERÇO, QUE ERA VOCÊ. SEU NASCIMENTO ENCHEU DE ALEGRIA O
CORAÇÃO MEU E DA MAMÃE. AGORA VOCÊ JÁ É MOCINHA, QUASE
CAPAZ DE VIVER SOZINHA. QUERO DIZER-LHE ALGUMAS COISAS
MUITO IMPORTANTES PARA O SEU BEM ESTAR FUTURO.

1. NUNCA COMECE O DIA SEM PEDIR QUE DEUS LHE DÊ PROTEÇÃO
E ORIENTAÇÃO.

2. NUNCA VÁ DORMIR SEM TER ESTUDADO A BÍBLIA.

3. SEJA SEMPRE SINCERA E HONESTA MESMO QUE PENSEM OU
FALEM MAL DE VOCÊ POR ISTO.

4. TIRE CADA DIA ALGUM TEMPO PARA, BEM A SÓS, MEDITAR NO
PASSADO, PRESENTE E FUTURO, E ENTÃO, DE JOELHOS, CONVERSAR
TODAS AS ALEGRIAS E TRISTEZAS, PLANOS E IDÉIAS, NO
[...] MELHOR [...] JESUS. (SE FIZER ISTO COM
SINCERIDADE, JESUS ESTARÁ JUNTINHO DE VOCÊ, DISTO TENHO CERTEZA). É MUITO
BOM LER ALGUM LIVRO DE E. WHITE, COMO O CAMINHO A
CRISTO, A MAIOR DE TODAS [...]

5. SEJA CASEIRA.

6. NUNCA FIQUE LONGE DE PESSOAS. NUNCA ENTRE NUM CARRO
OU CASA COM DESCONHECIDOS.

7. NÃO PENSE EM NAMORO. ISTO É PARA MAIS TARDE.

8. NUNCA PERMITA QUE ALGUM HOMEM LHE ACARICIE, APALPE OU

One week before Antonio's daughters left for Brazil, his wife smuggled
two sheets of paper to him so that he could write his farewell. Repro-
duced above is the first sheet of the letter that he thought might very
well be his last words to his daughters.

from Elena after she had received his scrap of paper.

Because of his prisoner status he had feared that she might encounter government opposition, and thus cause the children to be refused exit permits. But Elena kept him informed, as best she could, of the progress of negotiations for the tickets and plane reservations. At last the day came—Maria and Lucila would leave on Monday, February 9, about four months after their father had been imprisoned.

As he thought of his daughters being cared for by others—loving family members, but not their own parents—and of the problems they might face with no mother and no father to give tender counsel, his already-overburdened heart seemed to be physically bruised. So *much* he wanted to tell them. If only he had a few scraps of paper, perhaps he could record principles that he hoped would guide them for the rest of their lives. He knew he faced the definite possibility of never seeing them again in this world.

Elena, as always, anticipated his great need, his great desire. He could hardly comprehend the wonder of it all when, through what devious channels he might never know, she managed to smuggle to him two very small sheets of thin paper. In his mind he composed letter after letter, discarding this expression and that for the best way to convey his love and guidance. Not one word must be wasted; yet he must not overburden the children, facing as they were the separation from both parents. After a nearly sleepless night his mind cleared, and he was able to write swiftly and fluently. Now Maria and Lucila would have something of him to take into their uncertain future.

Antonio knew that the Sunday visit would be heartbreaking. He wanted to be cheerful for the sake of Elena and the girls, for he deeply felt the suffering that Elena must be enduring, devoted mother that she was. And his own relationship with the two little girls had always been unusually close. He knew that they would fight against leaving him, no matter what the danger. But how could any of this be expressed in the allowed five minutes, in mere shouts from the window across a courtyard.

Then another miracle occurred. The cell door clanged open. The prison commander stood framed in the opening.

"Antonio Silva, come with me!"

Antonio moved toward the door, dazed. He had seen Elena and Maria and Lucila approaching, as he gazed wistfully through the bars. Was he to be taken away and executed on the day before his little girls were to leave? Would he not even be allowed a final good-bye?

128

Brusquely the commander spoke. "You may go out into the prison yard and have a few moments with your wife and daughters," he informed Antonio, who followed him from the cell in a state of shock. Antonio tried to stammer his thanks, but the commander waved him to silence. And then he was in the yard with nothing between him and the three people he loved most on earth. He knew that he was not clean, though he always did his best. He knew that his hair was long and filthy and that he might be carrying disease germs. But his joy unutterable swept all those thoughts aside as he hugged the three of them, one by one, and choked out all the love and devotion which had been bottled up for so long.

He was determined not to weep for the sake of the children. But his eyes were swimming in tears, as were Elena's. Maria and Lucila sobbed with the hot, heartbroken tears of childhood.

"Don't you worry, my darlings. Jesus will take care of you. Remember all that you have been taught, and be true to God in everything you do," he whispered to them.

Then the dreaded summons—"Antonio Silva! Return to your cell!"

So much he wanted to say; so much he must leave unsaid—he could hardly tear his arms away from the clinging bodies of his children. But he knew that he must not jeopardize their lives by his disobedience. With dragging footsteps he made his way to the cell, where his friends had held a place for him at one of the windows.

He could see the soldiers shouting at Elena and Maria and Lucila to move faster. "Keep moving! Keep moving!" they shouted over and over.

But the three moved as slowly as they could without incurring punishment from the soldiers. They waved and waved and waved, over and over. Through the bars he waved his hand to them. Finally the three disappeared through the outside prison courtyard door. They were gone, perhaps forever, as far as Antonio Silva could see and hope.

Suddenly a little figure came flashing around the corner and through the gate again. It was Maria, waving and sending kisses to him. It seemed as though the child could not leave him. He was terrified for her, and the ache in his heart was so acute that he began to realize how human beings could die of a broken heart. Finally she too was gone.

His three friends understood his anguish. They understood that he must have some quiet time, if only a few minutes, to talk with God and to beg for emotional strength to endure what must be endured. God was good. After a few moments a kind of sad peace permeated his soul. In a sense the worst had happened, and he was no longer so fearful.

Later, in freedom, he asked Elena why she had not gone back to Brazil with the children. "Dear one, if you had to die here in this strange country, then I was determined to die with you," she had told him simply. "Whither thou goest, I will go." She had had to choose between her husband and her children, a cruel choice few women are called upon to make.

Knowing the plane schedule as he did, Antonio awakened very early in the morning, having slept very little. At six o'clock the jet should be leaving. How he hoped that the noise in the cell would not drown out the sound of the jet motors in their takeoff pattern directly over the prison. Listening intently, he heard, at first very faintly, then louder and louder, the unmistakable rumble of jet engines. He knew that his little girls were on the plane. He knew that a large part of his heart was on the plane with them. He knew that they would not lack for love among all the relatives in Brazil. But in a larger sense they were now homeless, his dear, dear little daughters.

During this period of extra nervous strain Elena had slipped a piece of paper in his clean towel which told him that in Lisbon the International Red Cross had announced that he had been released.

"Released!" he exclaimed to his friends. "Why, if that is the news being given out, and if everyone believes it, then the government here never has to let us go. They can simply say blandly that they have no prisoner with my name—and point to the Red Cross announcement."

He wondered if he had emotional reserve to withstand this new trial. Yet there were more to come. One day a clean-cut white man was thrown into the cell. His looks and manners strongly suggested that he was not a criminal. Pastor Silva watched him with interest, wondering at the story behind his imprisonment. Days passed, and he noticed that the man never received clean clothes. No relatives came to the courtyard. Was he alone in the world?

One day the man opened a conversation, "I'm an engineer," he told Antonio. "Do you know why I am here? I was in charge of a government project, building a dam. The president of this country was planning to visit the dam. I had received the word that his visit would take place on a day when I had planned to return to the city to visit my family. So I sent them a message saying that I would have to postpone my visit because the president would come to inspect the dam that day and I must be present.''

A bitter half-smile twisted his lips. ''The telegram was turned over to the police. I was accused of plotting to reveal the whereabouts of the president so that he could be assassinated.''

The engineer's face revealed his suffering. ''My family know that I am here. I got word to them that this was where I was being taken. But none of them has come to see me in the courtyard or to bring me clean clothes. What could have happened to them?''

Several weeks later, through one of the guards less unfriendly than others, the engineer learned that his family had indeed come to the prison to inquire about him and to make arrangments to care for his needs. Blandly the prison commander had replied to them, ''We have no one by that name here.''

When the engineer heard this, he was filled with despair. Pastor Silva and his friends also were crushed. They all knew how this kind of government could simply make people disappear without a trace and claim forever that it had never heard of them. Pastor Silva remembered again, as he had so many other times, the stories his parents had told him of his relatives in the Old Country—the disappearances, the lack of explanations, the sorrow, and the bewilderment of never really knowing all that had happened.

Just when the gloom was darkest, the Lord sent another ray of light. How, Pastor Silva never knew, but one of the other prisoners had managed to have a small New Testament, which also contained the Psalms, smuggled in to him. Antonio had been afraid for Elena's safety should she try such a scheme. He had not wanted her to attempt it. But oh, how he had longed to read the beautiful, comforting Scriptures. He knew many psalms by memory, and he had repeated them over and over. Nevertheless, to borrow the little Testament and read over and over the texts which meant so much to him was joy unutterable.

> ''God is our refuge and strength,
> a very present help in trouble.
> Therefore will not we fear,
> though the earth be removed, and though
> the mountains be carried into the midst of the sea;
> Though the waters thereof roar and be troubled,
> though the mountains shake with the swelling thereof. Selah.

There is a river, the streams whereof shall make glad
the city of God, the holy place of the tabernacles of the most High.
God is in the midst of her; she shall not be moved: God shall help her,
and that right early.
The heathen raged, the kingdoms were moved:
he uttered his voice, the earth melted.
The Lord of hosts is with us; the God of Jacob is our refuge. Selah.
Come, behold the works of the Lord, what desolations he hath made
in the earth.
He maketh wars to cease unto the end of the earth;
he breaketh the bow, and cutteth the spear in sunder;
he burneth the chariot in the fire.
Be still, and know that I am God:
I will be exalted among the heathen,
I will be exalted in the earth.
The Lord of hosts is with us;
The God of Jacob is our refuge. Selah."
   Psalm 46

And then there were the powerful words of Psalm 91:

"He that dwelleth in the secret place of the most High
shall abide under the shadow of the Almighty.
I will say of the Lord, He is my refuge and my fortress:
my God; in Him will I trust.
Surely he shall deliver thee from the snare of the fowler,
and from the noisome pestilence.
He shall cover thee with his feathers, and under his wings
shalt thou trust: his truth shall be thy shield and buckler.
Thou shalt not be afraid for the terror by night;
nor for the arrow that flieth by day;
Nor for the pestilence that walketh in darkness;
nor for the destruction that wasteth at noonday.
A thousand shall fall at thy side, and ten thousand at thy right hand;
but it shall not come nigh thee.
Only with thine eyes shalt thou behold and see the reward of the wicked.
Because thou hast made the Lord, which is my refuge,
even the most High, thy habitation;
There shall no evil befall thee,
neither shall any plague come nigh thy dwelling.
For he shall give his angels charge over thee, to keep thee
in all thy ways. They shall bear thee up in their hands,
lest thou dash thy foot against a stone.
Thou shalt tread upon the lion and adder:

132

the young lion and the dragon shalt thou trample under feet.
Because he hath set his love upon me, therefore will I deliver him:
I will set him on high, because he hath known my name.
He shall call upon me, and I will answer him: I will be with him
in trouble; I will deliver him, and honour him.
With long life will I satisfy him, and shew him my salvation.''

Other psalms and other parts of the New Testament were a comfort, but somehow these two could calm his soul as nothing else could.

Sometimes, for further comfort, he would whistle softly to himself the old and familiar hymns that had had such meaning for him all the days of his youth and of his gospel ministry. The beautiful tunes carried him back to many memorable evangelistic efforts, to the glory of a large congregation singing their hearts out for God, to the comfort and reassurance of family worship with the three he loved most—his ''girls.''

One song, though, he could not whistle. He could not even think of it without the hot tears springing unbidden to his eyes.

He had heard it in the beautiful Stadthalle in Vienna, Austria, at the time of the General Conference session, just a few months before he was imprisoned. Pastor C. D. Brooks had sung it with unmatched eloquence. To Antonio's sad heart it seemed as though he had heard it on another planet far removed from that dismal cell. The words, even when he had heard them in the joy of attending the world session and in fellowship with so many other believers, had gone straight to his heart. Now, they leaped to his mind, and his heavy heart seemed bruised as with a hammer:

''As the Father hath sent me,
So send I you.

So send I you to labor unrewarded,
To serve unpaid, unloved, unsought, unknown,
To bear rebuke, to suffer scorn and scoffing—
So send I you to toil for me alone.

So send I you to loneliness and longing,
With heart ahung'ring for the loved and known,
Forsaking home and kindred, friend and dear one—
So send I you to know my love alone.

So send I you to leave your Life's ambition,
To die to dear desire, self-will resign.
To labor long and love where men revile you;
So send I you to lose your life in mine.

So send I you to hearts made hard by hatred,
To eyes made blind because they will not see,
To spend, tho it be blood—to spend and spare not—
So send I you to taste of Calvary.

As the Father hath sent me,
So send I you.''

He had wanted, above all else, to be worthy of such words, as he listened on that bright and beautiful day in Vienna. He had prayed that God would make him a minister fit to follow in the footsteps of Christ.

''But, Lord, I did not understand then what it meant to suffer as you suffered. Now I understand more. Oh, I beg You, give me the strength to withstand whatever is in store for me,'' he prayed out of the depths of his suffering.

Throughout this dark period he did not give up his feeling of responsibility for the Lord's work in that sad country. He spent long hours wondering what would be best for both the nationals and expatriate workers. Finally he sent word to Elena, via the tiny rolled-up papers in the towel hem, that he felt it best for all the overseas workers to return to their homelands. He had put off the conclusion as long as possible, knowing that the Lord's work would move much more slowly in the future. Although he had tried to qualify the national workers as fully and as fast as possible, he felt that they were still not ready to take over completely.

Elena soon communicated to him that the workers were obtaining their exit permits one by one and leaving. Later Pastor Silva would learn that one very loyal Portuguese pastor told Elena, ''I will not leave this country unless and until Pastor Silva leaves also. I will not leave him here in prison.'' And so he stayed. Only later would Antonio know of the immense comfort he had been to Elena and the wife of the publishing secretary. The pastor had to stay a few days here and a few days there keeping forever on the move, or he himself would have been arrested. Somehow the Lord shielded him, and he stayed one jump ahead of the searching soldiers.

134

Through these bleak days the devil besieged the four men with yet more trial. If they felt depressed, almost immediately thoughts of self-doubt and failure flooded their minds: "You're a fine Christian!" the insinuating voice would whisper. "Aren't you something—to talk about faith in God and try to tell other people to have faith, when deep down in your own heart you know how despondent you are. What makes you think that God is going to do anything for such a worm as you? And if He really does love you as you claim, why are you so sad?"

But each time, when the darkness seemed almost total, a ray of light penetrated. One ray came in the form of a little rolled-up message from Elena telling Antonio that the Brazilian government was working very hard for his release. Elena was able to inform him that the government of Brazil had sent message after message demanding that he be released immediately, but the local government ignored the messages.

Later he would learn that Elena knew positively that the messages had been sent from Brazil because the daughter of one of the church members worked in the office of the Minister of the Interior. When a message came regarding his case, she faithfully reported it to her mother, who informed Elena. Even though the Brazilian embassy had closed, the home government tirelessly worked for the release of Pastor Silva and the publishing secretary. Its citizens were not abandoned.

"Listen to this!" Pastor Silva whispered to his companions, after reading one of Elena's notes. "My wife says that the International Red Cross is working for our release and so is the Euro-Africa Division of the General Conference—and the General Conference itself! Surely something will happen now."

But nothing happened.

Pastor Silva sensed dimly that Elena must be moving heaven and earth to keep all these people interested in his release and that of his companions. He knew that she must be putting herself in constant danger for his sake. Surely the effort would be successful. He went through short periods of euphoria, when he felt that at any moment the cell door would be flung wide and he would hear those longed-for words, "Antonio Silva! You are free!"

But the words never came. Often, as he prayed, he felt that God had indeed heard him; but that the answer was No. He remembered that while God always wants to answer our requests as we might wish, sometimes circumstances are such that we must accept a No or a Wait. Was this the case here? Did he now need to pray that his heart be made willing to accept any answer that God might give?

When they were well into the fifth month of imprisonment, for the first time Pastor Silva and the publishing secretary gave voice to what had been at the back of their minds ever since the terrible Friday when they had been thrown into the packed cell.

"If," said Pastor Silva tentatively on one hot, endless afternoon, "God does not see fit to release us, then that must mean that our work on earth for Him, as we have known it, is finished."

Both of them sat in silence for a few moments. "But do you think that God would plan that our lives should end in a foreign prison?" his fellow Brazilian asked over the lump in his throat.

"I don't think it is ever God's plan for his people to suffer," Pastor Silva assured him. "I simply believe that the devil brings all the suffering and the sadness in his power upon those who love God. If God always intervened to prevent this, it would be impossible for us to know whether we serve God out of pure love, or because we think our commitment will protect us."

It was hard, though, as the days went on and the two other friends also voiced their inner feelings. They were not in a state of discouragement, for all four felt an abiding sense of the presence of God more distinctly than before. Perhaps *resignation* expresses their attitude during this period.

They did not know how long the food arrangement could continue; they did know that without it they would not live long. Their weakened bodies could not withstand the lack of rest and cleanliness, the continual fear and tension, without the food they were given from home. Later, after his release, Pastor Silva would learn that according to one reliable source, more than 3000 Jehovah's Witnesses died in prisons during those first few months, and many from other religious sects died also. Death, then, was a possibility that must be faced.

During this time, over and over, Antonio thought of his parents. The old stories of persecution, work camps, starvation, and death beat through his brain relentlessly. Moreover, he could not forget that his mother had asked him not to return to this country after his furlough. "You were not a loving and obedient son," someone seemed to whisper. "If your parents die of grief, you are to blame." It seemed useless to protest silently in the never-ending dialogue that he had felt a duty to God. His thoughts churned endlessly.

136

One day as Pastor Silva was leaning against the cell wall, he looked down at his publishing secretary lying on the floor, doubled up into the tiny available space. Pastor Silva's heart lurched suddenly. "Why, he looks almost as though he were dead," he said to himself. "He looks so thin, so pale, and so dirty. Can this be the same cheerful, husky, nice-looking man whom I have had as a friend for so long?"

Suddenly he realized that he must look much the same. He had not had access to a mirror through all the long months of imprisonment. He wondered how Elena and the little girls had managed to act so natural with him, when it was obvious that he must have been a frightening sight.

When his heart was heaviest, he turned his thoughts to a message which Elena had sent him earlier. Probably she had sent it as an encouragement, for she told him that she had secured air tickets for the two of them, and for the publishing secretary and his wife and small daughter. Surely, surely this was tangible evidence that someday he and his companions would be free. He dreamed of the takeoff—of the plane bounding into the blue sky, of the terror and nightmare all behind him. He dreamed that he would be free. He would be free.

Elena began sending messages of even greater hope and encouragement. For the first time, it seemed to him, she had definite information regarding their release, or at least definite hope that this would come about. He had waited for the opening of the door and the announcement for so long that now it had lost its touch of reality.

"I wonder," he said one day to his friends, "if my dear wife is suffering from the strain of this terrible thing and isn't completely aware of the import of the messages she is sending."

They pondered for a moment.

"Perhaps she isn't being given proper information," the publishing secretary said.

"Or maybe she knows we have such a great need to hear encouraging things that this is why she tells me what she does," Pastor Silva remarked. It was difficult to understand it all.

Then information was passed throughout the cell that a severe food shortage existed in the country, especially there in the city. Pastor Silva had thought that his life had hit the lowest point when his children had left the country; now he found that it could go even lower. He could not sleep, wondering what Elena's true condition was. Yet she and his friend's wife continued to bring them food.

A Change for the Better

Pastor Silva felt another change in himself as the days dragged by, probably as the result of his physical, mental, and emotional strains. At first he had seen himself in a totally different category than the large bulk of prisoners. "They are criminals, and I am innocent. Of course I will be released," he had assured himself. Now it seemed to him that the difference between him and the other prisoners was very small. They all looked equally dirty, unkempt, and malnourished. They all seemed equally hopeless. Time seemed to run in a blur—confused, distorted—sweeping them all along with no beginnings and no endings. This packed, reeking cell full of seething humanity comprised the bounds of his life.

When thoughts plagued him that he would be better off dead, he always argued vigorously. "I am going to be with Elena and Maria and Lucila. I shall live," he responded over and over, though sometimes he found it difficult to believe his own words.

He felt a vast kinship, a great and overwhelming pity for all his cellmates. Everyone in this inhuman situation was enmeshed in a tragedy of one sort or another. Everyone had loved ones who waited somewhere, some praying but all longing for the release of the prisoners. Even if Elena did secure his release, would it be fair for him to leave all these other men, these hopeless souls, so lost and alone? He no longer felt separate and on a higher plane. Perhaps it would be better for them all to die together as they had lived. When these thoughts came, he banished them with thoughts of freedom. But such despairing thoughts tormented him during the long, uncomfortable nights.

Conditions in the cell were now rapidly deteriorating. One evening

138

at about eight o'clock shooting was heard on the outside of the prison.

Suddenly a powerful blast shook the building. "A bomb must have been dropped!" Pastor Silva shouted to his companions. All the lights went out, leaving the packed cell in total darkness. The blackness induced such a feeling of suffocation that, for a few moments, Antonio wondered if everyone would go mad with panic. Then, as the sound of shooting and the machine-gun fire picked up in intensity, the prisoners shouted to one another, "Lie down on the floor! Lie down on the floor! You can be killed by stray bullets coming through the bars!"

But there was not enough floor space for them all to lie flat. Bodies were piled upon bodies. Arms and legs kicked and flailed in panic. For the long, long hour that the heaviest of the shooting lasted, the prisoners did not know what was happening or what would happen to them.

In Pastor Silva's imagination, he constructed a new war in this already war-torn country. "Can the insurgents, whoever they may be, attempt to open the prison and free us?" he asked himself. If that were the case, he wondered if any would leave the prison alive.

Finally the shooting tapered off, though occasional bursts of machine-gun fire continued throughout the night. When dawn came, the terrified prisoners tried to find out the cause of the disturbance. But no one would answer their questions. The guards who took them to breakfast were stony faced and silent. The prisoners could only conjecture regarding imaginary wars and imaginary invasions by other countries.

When night came, to their horror the same scenario took place, depriving them of yet another night of sleep. The packed, reeking cell was now full of exhausted men whose tempers were at flash point. But they were yet to endure a third night of fighting, still with no information as to the cause. Pastor Silva was no longer concerned for himself; he was consumed with fear for Elena. His companions suffered in the same way for their loved ones. What was happening in the city?

Eventually they received a crumb of information. It seemed that part of the national army had split off from the main body and had endeavored to attack the prison, probably with the intent of releasing the prisoners. But they did not achieve their objective. Later, when he was free, Pastor Silva learned that some parts of the city had been under exceedingly heavy fire, and many people were killed. For weeks the sound of machine guns became a nightly occurrence.

As the cell continued to fill with prisoners, standing room became even more scarce. In desperation, the prisoners determined that not one more man would be allowed to enter and use more of the oxygen and overtax the incredibly inadequate "sanitary facility."

Thus, when a guard tried to open the door to press yet another body inside, they would form an impenetrable wall with their bodies, leaning with their full weight against the door, making it impossible to admit the new prisoner. The guards would retaliate by beating the prisoners near the door with their clubs, but the exhausted, desperate men no longer cared what happened to them. Hopeless as they now were, the blows that were rained onto their emaciated forms seemed not to be felt.

The thin thread of sanity began to snap in one man after another. One night a terrible commotion broke out from a nearby cell.

"Kill me! Kill me!" shrieked a prisoner, over and over. "I can't stand it. I want to die! I want to die!"

Eventually guards came in, and Pastor Silva and his friends could hear the sounds of the unmerciful beating which reduced the suffering soul to a heap of quiet sobs.

The nights became endurance contests, with now over 200 men in the cell. Some would jump to their feet at three or four in the morning and begin long, detailed, incoherent "addresses" while the others shouted their hatred; eventually the disturbed men were quieted with force.

Pastor Silva noted one night, through the flickering of the pale light bulbs, a young man who had jumped to his feet. He suddenly stretched out his arm as though it were a guitar. Using his other arm to strum his "guitar," he began to sing in a loud, quavering voice. Others in the cell shouted for him to be quiet. But he went on and on, oblivious to everything but the "music" he was making. This "music" evidently took his mind outside the hopelessness and misery of his physical being.

During the early days of their imprisonment Pastor Silva and his friends had talked endlessly. They had explored every possible way that freedom might come. They had recited all the texts they could remember, over and over. They had reviewed all the doctrines of the church. But now they found themselves becoming more and more silent and listless. Even the effort of speech seemed not worth the while. During the days they stood against the walls or squatted in any small space they could find. Sometimes the men standing would become so exhausted and sleepy that they would collapse on the bodies already on the floor and continue to sleep, oblivious to the angry threats of those upon whom they had fallen.

Violence had become a daily occurrence.

"Look at that man," the publishing secretary whispered to Pastor Silva one day.

"That man" was enormously large and strong. He had been thrown into the cell only a few days before. His body had not yet begun to show the effects of imprisonment under these conditions. He was beating on the cell door with all the weight of his body. "Let me out! Let me out!" he screamed hoarsely, over and over and over. Though, from the outside, the guard threatened him and commanded him to cease, the prisoner continued his beating on the door until the nerves of all in the cell were strained to breaking.

Suddenly the guard threw open the door. Quick as a wink the man stooped to the floor and flung a handful of human excrement into the guard's face. At once he was dragged from the cell by other guards and beaten unconscious—then brought back and flung into the midst of the packed cell.

Prisoners began desperate plans to escape. Some hid under the cement tables at mealtimes. One morning Pastor Silva's cell heard that about twenty prisoners from an upper floor had cut the bars of one of the windows—using what tool, no one seemed to know. They had slipped down, having tied their clothes together as a rope. The guards had not discovered the plot in time, perhaps due to the heavy rains which fell that night. It was rumored that most of these men had escaped. At night the sound of guards shooting at prisoners attempting to escape became a common occurrence.

When the long lines of prisoners were taken back and forth from the dining room, it became not unusual for one or two to slip out of line and run through the hall with a swiftness born of desperation. Sometimes when stopped by guards, they would shout, "I am a mechanic from the prison garage. You had better not interfere with me!" Of course their pitiful ruse was always discovered.

One prisoner, though, did escape in a most ingenious way. With a small bit of paper folded in his hands, he left the dining room line, merged into the background, and reappeared in the front of the prison, claiming to be a messenger. He very smoothly told the guards that he had delivered his message. They sent him on through the gate, and only when he had been given a ride by a passing motorist and had

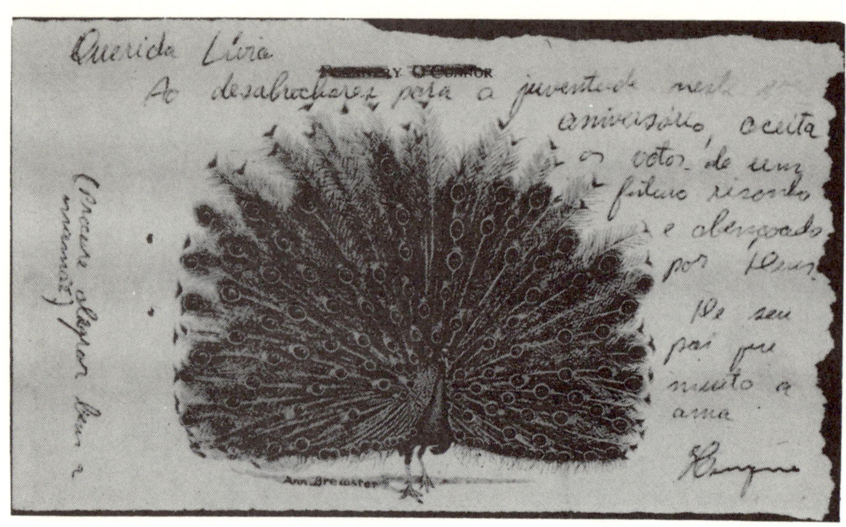

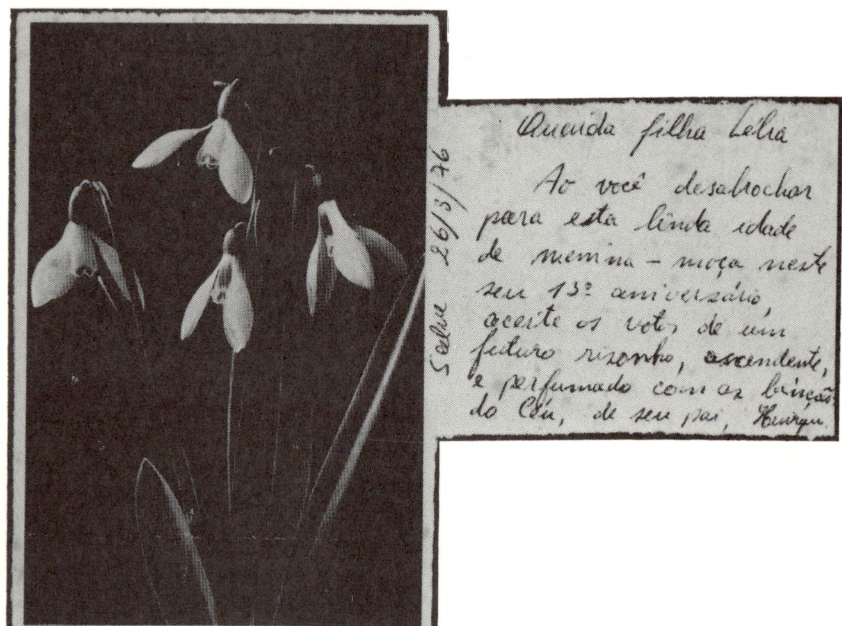

Birthday cards for his two daughters consisted of extracts from old magazines that symbolized beauty and what might yet be. The peacock was sent to his elder daughter, the flowers to his younger.

disappeared did his subterfuge come to light. Some of the guards were punished cruelly for that mistake. All the prison, however, alerted by the "grapevine," rejoiced that at least one man was now free.

Riots became a frightening part of the prison experience. These were especially terrifying to the four friends, for they were aware only too well that deaths occur in prison riots. Also it was difficult to maintain loyalty to God and to principle while maintaining some kind of rapport with the others in the cell—so that the four would not be murdered in their sleep.

On one occasion, as they were eating, some of the more aggressive prisoners jumped onto the tables and shouted, "We will not return to the cells! We will not be treated any longer as animals! We will die before we will go back!"

The entire room took up the chant. The crescendo of male voices became louder and more menacing. Pastor Silva and his companions looked at one another in silent entreaty. They prayed to God that somehow their lives would be spared. Would the guards come into the dining room with guns, shooting at the tightly packed mass of humanity?

The guards screamed and shouted back to the prisoners. Hour after hour went by. Each moment the four friends expected to die, either at the hands of the prisoners or by the guns of the guards. But miraculously, no physical violence took place, only verbal violence.

When both sides were exhausted, and no progress was being made, the prison commander arrived. Soothingly he promised better treatment for all. The exhausted prisoners marched back to their cells. The "better treatment" never did materialize.

Whenever a riot occurred, the prisoners were punished by being starved for several days. After the dining room incident, no food of any kind was permitted for forty-eight hours. When the weakened prisoners were finally taken out for their meager breakfast, all the fight had gone out of them. The four friends had not been permitted to receive their food from home. They suffered with the others.

During this brutal time Pastor Silva would sometimes see his three companions squatting near the floor, with their heads bowed silently between their knees. He knew that they were holding back the tears—sometimes unable to hold them back—wondering if God indeed still loved them. Sometimes God seemed very far away.

Yet there were precious moments when His presence seemed almost tangible. One day Lamentations 3:22, 23 came to Pastor Silva's mind: "It is of the Lord's mercies that we are not consumed, because his compassions fail not. They are new every morning." He could still feel profound gratitude that he was still alive.

But then he thought of Matthew 5, wherein God's followers are admonished to rejoice when they are cast into prison for His sake. Somehow he could not fathom that text in this setting. All too easily he had used this as sermon material when he was free, well-fed, well-dressed, with all of his life before him. But emotionally he was unable now to accept the text as fully as he wished.

"You know," Pastor Silva said to his companions one day, "when we first were brought here, I was thinking all the time of only one thing—when the four of us would be released. I never really thought of the other prisoners. I never thought of the fact that they wished to be free as much as I do. But now—when an occasional prisoner really is released, I find that I can rejoice for him, even though I am still here."

"Yes," the publishing secretary replied, "in a strange sort of way, these sad men seem like brothers now. We have all suffered together."

After a few moments Pastor Silva continued quietly, "True brotherhood may be found only in suffering; Jesus taught us that."

As the months dragged by, Pastor Silva realized that his mind had accommodated itself to the fact that his "home" was a little piece of old, dirty, torn blanket, and one third of a square meter of space. This had more reality for him than the car that he had left in the driveway of his home. How could this be? And yet it was so.

Later, in freedom, he shuddered at the thought of even touching that dirty, filthy piece of blanket which had been his world. But at that time he felt the affection for it that a little child feels to whom a piece of candy has more value than a check for $1000.

In order to keep his mind from dwelling on the apparent hopelessness of the situation, Pastor Silva made a conscious effort to take a trip in memory back through his entire life. Sometimes his imagination was so vivid that he seemed to be standing in front of one of his congregations in Brazil, recognizing every one of the members and calling each by name. He remembered incidents in the lives of these parishioners. Then he would be startled back to reality by the shouts and screams of his cellmates.

Sometimes he imagined himself in his little VW, driving on the roads of Brazil. The curves, the trees, the mountains, the houses were as real in his mind as though he were looking at photographs. But sometimes he would become concerned when his daydreams became too vivid, lest he lose his hold on reality and slip over the brink.

"I must be alert at all times for whatever emergency may arise," he told himself. "God needs me in the best mental state I can be in." He still maintained a strong feeling of protectiveness toward the other three and felt that he must encourage and help them in any possible way. Their attitude toward him was the same—protective and caring.

Often he reviewed various actions that he had taken. Had he made proper decisions there in his cell? He remembered when he had felt so strongly impressed that all the expatriate workers should leave this country. He had prayed almost without ceasing for three days and three nights. He had talked it over with his companions, and finally, based on material he remembered having read in Ellen White's books, he had advised his workers to go. This was probably the hardest decision he had had to make, because of the effect on God's work.

Pastor Silva's quick mind was always thinking of new ways in which the imprisonment could be made easier, ways in which the suffocating sense of captivity could be lessened. In the dining room, packed as he was within the mass of humanity, he began to study the faces of the guards, always hoping to find one or two less depraved or brutal than the others. His purpose was not to bribe these men or to ask for favors that were improper, but only to alleviate, to some extent, his condition and that of his friends.

One day he overheard one of the guards congratulating another on the birth of a baby boy. "This is the opportunity we've been waiting for," he told his publishing secretary. On a tiny scrap of paper he sent the guard's name to Elena, with instructions as to what he hoped she might be able to do. She understood. In some way she ascertained the address of the guard and his wife, prepared some baby clothes and delivered them at the house with Pastor Silva's name as donor. Whatever the culture or belief, Pastor Silva was banking on the fact that the birth of a new baby is a very special event. He was not wrong.

Several times workers from the mission had tried to get close enough to the bars to pass a Bible to the four companions. On one occasion Pastor Silva had his arms stretched as far as possible outside the window bars, reaching, reaching for the Bible held out to him by a church member. Just as his fingertips touched the precious object, a guard angrily knocked it from the hands of the giver, and ordered him to leave the prison yard immediately. To have this dearest of treasures snatched away when victory had seemed certain, was almost more than Pastor Silva could bear.

One day, though, when Elena brought his clean clothes, she noticed that the guard examining the clothes was the one to whom she had taken the baby gifts. She had prayed earnestly, she later told Antonio, that this would be the case and had brought along a small Bible in the hope and faith that this would work out. Quickly she took Antonio's clothes to this guard.

"Clothes for Pastor Antonio Silva," she said.

His eyes met hers as he "examined" the clothes. He could not help having felt the small Bible, but he gave no sign of having done so. With no hesitation he brought the package into the cell.

What rejoicing there was among the four when they realized that at long last they had the Word of God—both Old and New Testaments—in their own hands again. They wept tears of joy and gratitude.

"We must make up a schedule, so that we will all have equal time to study our Bible," Pastor Silva announced. "I feel as though I could sit down and read it from cover to cover without stopping!"

During the days which followed, the Bible was enjoyed not only by the four companions, but by many of the other prisoners who had come to respect Pastor Silva and his friends. They discovered new truths, new aspects of life that had never occurred to them before.

When Elena, using the same method, was able to send a copy of *Life at Its Best,* by Ellen White, it seemed to Pastor Silva that his cup indeed was running over with joy. He was no longer a mere prisoner of the iron bars and the packed cell—his spirit was free. As he read the precious promises and beautiful descriptions in that book, his soul, so long stunted and impoverished, felt as though it were flowering. It was for his soul, he thought, the springtime of release after the winter of agony.

Moreover, the lines of communication with Elena seemed to be working well these days. In tiny script she wrote, "The president of the Euro-Africa Division, the president of the General Conference, and one of the secretaries of the General Conference have all written letters of encouragement to me. It means so much to know that others are sharing our great trial."

One day in his clean clothes Antonio found very thin pieces of paper that were so precious he could not hold back the tears. He recognized the handwriting of Maria and Lucila. His girls, safely in

Brazil, lovingly cared for by relatives, wanted him to know that he was never out of their thoughts. He read the messages over and over until he had memorized them. Then he continued to read them, day after day, until the fragile paper was almost worn out from his handling of it. Whatever might come, the love of God and of his wife and children were a constant bulwark against despair.

In all her messages to him regarding the future, Elena had never once said, "IF you are released from prison." Always she wrote "WHEN you are released." Her strong faith was a rock. Now she sent him a message that his future employment in Brazil was already under consideration. "I have heard that you will be asked to be the pastor of the large church in C———" was the welcome news.

He held the bit of paper in his hand and marveled. Here he was, apparently as far from being released as he had been the first day that he was imprisoned. His health was precarious, his spirits sometimes low, his emotions drained. Yet Elena and his brethren were sure that before long he would be pastoring this lovely church. Dare he allow himself to believe that such a thing could come to pass? Dare he hope, only to have his hopes dashed to the ground once again? As he thought it over for hours, he began to feel that if the Lord would be so gracious as to permit his release, what he would most like to do would indeed be pastoral work. He longed for contact with members on a one-to-one basis. Administration no longer held the appeal for him that once it had. He prayed that he could spend his days in personal evangelism and in strengthening the faith of God's people.

In spite of the encouragement from the Bible and *Life at Its Best*, and from Elena's optimistic messages, conditions in the cell were so intolerable by March that Antonio sensed that something must happen soon or all would be lost. Emotionally and mentally he was fighting a hard battle; he was steadily deteriorating physically. He conveyed his apprehension to Elena. Immediately she returned a bit of paper with the news that a "friend" (unnamed) was working for his release. He did not dare to hope again, but hoped nonetheless.

Later, in freedom, he would learn that the "friend" was a citizen of another African country with a high position in the United Nations delegation in that city. He was also a commander in the armed forces of his country. Though not an Adventist, he had asked that the ministers in prison pray for him.

"Pray for HIM?" was Pastor Silva's instinctive response. "Why, he is a free man and high in influential circles. Does he want humble prisoners to intercede with God for him?''

But instantly he regretted his reaction. The truth swept over him that no earthly position or advantage can provide spiritual security. The latter comes only in a personal relationship with God.

Later he would learn that this same man had offered to give Elena money if she were in need. He would also learn that the General Conference had tried through this same African government to effect his release and that of his companions. But it was to no avail. Nonetheless, as the situation progressed (and as events became clearer in the future) Pastor Silva would learn that this ''friend'' whom he never met had done more than anyone else—had been more effective than anyone else—in securing the release of himself and the two other pastors.

When March was nearly over, two more prisoners were packed into the cell. One man, Pastor Silva noticed, seemed far superior to the general run of prisoners. On the second morning, when he had made a slight adjustment to the trauma, he made his way to Pastor Silva and, in English, asked if he were the Seventh-day Adventist pastor who was in charge of the gospel work in this country.

Upon being assured that this was the case—and Pastor Silva's astonishment was mirrored on his face as he wondered just why the new prisoner would know this—the man bowed his head.

''I come from another African country,'' he whispered. ''I am a commercial builder of houses, and have been here in this country following my trade. But someone contacted me, asking that I do all I could to get you out of prison. I made approaches to various officials, but I was reported, and now I have been imprisoned also. When I crossed the border, the guards became suspicious and would not let me return to my home. Here I am. But I have many friends in this city, and we are prepared to pay any sum for your release and for mine.''

Pastor Silva shook his head, unable to organize his whirling thoughts. Could he really have heard what the man had just said? Moreover, the speaker was so confident, so full of energy, so undefeated that he was like a fresh, strong wind. A tiny sprig of hope burst into bloom in Antonio's heart.

''Truly,'' his new friend declared, ''we will be released within the next few days. I do not lie to you. It will happen.''

Going on, he outlined a plan whereby the wives of the four men would be taken out of the country by car, first to a friendly country, and then his associates would effect the release of the four Adventists and himself. They would all rendezvous in a friendly country.

Dazed, but grasping at straws, Pastor Silva painstakingly wrote all the details on bits of paper and smuggled them out to Elena.

But the hopes of all were dashed, when, on the night of April 1, a guard threw open the cell door and shouted the names of Pastor Silva, his publishing secretary, and the national pastor. He did not call the name of the national colporteur.

"Get your things and come with me," he ordered brusquely.

What could be happening? What was it all about? Were they actually going to be released? If so, why wasn't the new friend's name called?

With the guard shouting at them to hurry, they picked up their pieces of ragged blanket and tried to hide their Bible and the Ellen White book under them. Suddenly they realized that they would be leaving their dear brother, the national colporteur, behind. He was now truly a brother, after all the suffering they had endured together. It seemed to Pastor Silva that he could not bear to leave this young man alone in the cell with the vicious, rough men, with no one who cared for him.

He threw his arms around his young friend, and with tears in his eyes said, "Please be faithful until Jesus comes. Here—" and impulsively he lifted his ragged, dirty scrap of blanket and revealed the books—"I want you to take the Bible and *Life at Its Best*. You will need them, for you are alone now."

Weeping, the young colporteur clung to him.

"We'll meet in heaven, if we never meet again on this earth," Pastor Silva promised. One by one, the three men embraced the young colporteur. Then they made their way among the tightly packed men in the cell, the target of curious stares and murmurs.

Pastor Silva never learned, even in freedom, what had happened to the man in the prison who had been so confident that he could effect their release.

As they followed the guard down the corridor and into the prison commander's office for paperwork—always necessary in these countries—it dawned on Pastor Silva that maybe they were not going to be released after all. But still, any change must surely be for the better.

"May we have our belts and ties?" he inquired courteously.

After a long wait, these were brought. An encouraging sign.

They did not dare ask many questions. Finally it was indicated to them that they were to be transferred to another prison. Though their hopes for freedom were again dashed, Pastor Silva felt that the move was an answer to prayer. He had become desperate when the water supply in the cell had begun to fail. The sanitary hole could not be washed. The stench and filth were indescribable. He had sent Elena a message saying that if he and the others were not to be given freedom, could they be put into a better prison? Later he would learn that Elena had worked hard on this, and now her efforts were bearing fruit.

But he could not leave without Elena knowing where he was going. He addressed the guards again. "Will you please phone my wife and tell her where we have been taken?" he pleaded.

They nodded affirmatively, their faces impassive. He did not know whether they would do this, and the uncertainty was another source of torment.

Again there was the hurried walk down the corridor, down the steps, entry into a waiting car which started as soon as they were inside. For about half an hour during the drive, the three of them looked about hungrily, enjoying this small taste of the real world. It seemed more unreal than their own now did. It was as though reality were back in the prison cell with the mass of prisoners. How could there be happy, cheerful people on the streets, and lights, and families having their meal together, and cars everywhere?

Then suddenly they drew up in front of a huge building which they recognized as the state penetentiary. Pastor Silva's heart thudded. He wondered what conditions would be like here. Was this a move for the better or worse?

Suspense

First, the interminable paperwork had to be completed in the office of the prison commander. Then the three men were taken down a long hallway and put in separate cells on the same corridor. At least they would have some communication. Though this prison had twice as many inhabitants as it was built to accommodate, it was so far superior to the other that it seemed almost like a hotel. Pastor Silva found that he would have to sleep on the cement floor under the bed of another prisoner; but since he could stretch his body out full length, this was luxury unimaginable.

Moreover, the prisoners in that section were allowed to leave their cells at will and to walk up and down the corridors. "I can't believe it!" Pastor Silva said to himself as he took advantage of this liberty. "Surely they can't mean to give us this much freedom!"

That first night he walked for hours, up and down, up and down, reveling in the simple joy of freedom of movement. Could anyone ask for more out of life? But he found that his legs, so long unused, were stiff and would not move rapidly. Also, he had continued to have great trouble with swelling in his feet and legs. This kept walking from being a complete pleasure. But he walked. As the days went on, the swelling began to disappear.

On the next morning he learned from the other prisoners that once a day all prisoners could receive food from home. Now if only Elena had been told of his whereabouts, he was sure that she would be there with food—AND SHE WAS!

The guards had kept their word. They had phoned.

The blessings of this new prison seemed endless. Newspapers were allowed. Antonio could learn what was going on in the world, something he had been deprived of knowing for so many months. Some prisoners even had small radios and were able to pick up broadcasts from long distances. It was, to Pastor Silva, as though he had landed on another planet. He had so long been without these amenities of life that he felt as though he had discovered a field of diamonds.

But more delights were in store. The prison had a large yard, including a soccer field, which was kept open during daylight hours. Slowly the three friends began to put themselves on a routine of running and jogging, though at first, in their weakened condition, they could manage only a few yards. As they persisted, however, their strength began to return. New vigor changed their skin, so pale and sick looking, into a healthier tinge.

As if this were not enough, the food in this prison, while definitely substandard, was far superior to that in the prison they had left. Pastor Silva felt sad for the men in the old cell, so tightly packed together. He thanked God over and over again for having brought him to this place where human dignity could be maintained. But the bulk of his prayers centered on the men he had left, especially the young colporteur. His heart ached constantly for the boy. He prayed over and over for the latter's release and for the release of all innocent men in the old cell, including the man who had been so interested in effecting his and his friends' release.

A sweet peace filled his heart. He began to feel that if he must spend the rest of his days in captivity, then at least God had brought him to an endurable place. He was filled with gratitude and joy. When, without comment, a guard returned his watch to him soon after his arrival, he could not believe it. For six months he had had no way of knowing the exact time, since in the old cell watches were forbidden. Until this deprivation he had not realized how much civilized people depend upon a timepiece to order their activities. Knowing the time keeps one from feeling so disoriented, he thought.

When he and his friends, who every day spent their time together in the corridor and the yard, realized that they could glimpse their wives when they brought food each day, they felt that surely they were the most favored of men. No special permits were now needed for the bringing of food. Each time Elena appeared, however, Pastor Silva's heart ached for the young man whose prescription had kept them alive in the first prison. What was happening to him now?

On that first day Pastor Silva exclaimed excitedly, "Look! Our wives are only about twenty meters away, out there at the front gate.

152

We can see them plainly. They can see us waving to them and they can wave back.'' And that is what they did, day after day.

No longer did they have afternoon "visiting hours" twice a week as in the old prison; from time to time the prisoners were allowed five minutes to speak to their dear ones through the bars. With everyone shouting to be heard, Pastor Silva faced the same problems as formerly. He and Elena never really were able to hear one another. The frustration was the same as ever. Later, however, Antonio was unexpectedly given permission to meet Elena in the prison yard for a brief visit. Both were almost tongue-tied, with so much needing to be said. Their words tripped over one another.

"Do not despair, dearest. God is going to see that you are released," Elena assured him over and over. Questions tumbled from Antonio's lips. How were the girls getting along in Brazil? How were all the grandparents? What had happened to the other mission workers, the nationals? Was the work being carried forward at all? Did she have enough money? Was she getting enough to eat?

Her questions matched his. Did he feel better than he had felt in the old cell? Was the food she brought sufficient? Was the swelling gone from his feet and legs? Was he now able to sleep better? Were the new cellmates decent men?

The time they were allowed flew on wings, and much was left unsaid.

On that first day in the new prison, when the guard brought their food to them, the men very inconspicuously began searching for messages, for bits of rolled-up paper. Later Pastor Silva would learn that the guards had made it emphatically clear that absolutely no messages must go back and forth. Yet, since he had committed no crime and was totally innocent of wrongdoing—indeed, had not even been charged with wrongdoing—Pastor Silva continued to feel that he was not sinning by sending and receiving messages.

When he received his food, it was certainly not in the condition in which Elena prepared it, for to insure that no messages were sent, the guards pierced all the food with small iron rods. Miraculously, the messages for him were never discovered. The bits of rolled-up paper seemed to have a life of their own. They seemed almost able to hide themselves from the "divining rods."

One day a guard came striding through the corridor carrying a small mattress. "Antonio Silva!" he shouted, and when Antonio faced the corridor through the bars, the guard came to the cell and threw the mattress on the floor. "Your wife sent this," he growled, then turned and left.

Antonio could not comprehend for a moment. Was he now allowed to have a mattress, like a free human being? After all these months of trying to sleep on the hard cement floor, could this be happening? He wondered for a brief moment, if his sanity, which he had prayed so hard to preserve, had actually gone. But then he realized that all was well, that he was now the owner of a mattress. He placed it under the bed of the prisoner, where he had been assigned to sleep. Then he stretched out on it. Surely nothing in his subsequent life would ever feel as soft, as wonderful, as totally comforting as that bare little mattress.

"I feel almost well and free," he whispered to himself. As the nights came and went, his sore, tired, and aching body began to relax and heal itself.

As he became acquainted with the other prisoners, Pastor Silva learned many sad stories. First, he discovered that many prisoners from his old prison, who had been taken from the cell and supposedly freed, were now prisoners here. To each one he said, "I am so sorry. I thought you were now free."

Moreover, he gradually became somewhat acquainted with missionaries in this prison who were members and leaders of other Protestant groups in this country. For instance, there were several European and American missionaries from the Nazarene Church. Somehow friends in the United States had been able to procure for them a tiny electric stove. How they had gotten permission to keep it in their cell, he could not imagine. They were able to cook for themselves small amounts of food far superior to the prison diet.

All these missionaries had been arrested much earlier than had Pastor Silva. They seemed to have no hope or expectation of release. Realizing this, Antonio's spirits for a time began to sink again, but then he recounted to himself the many blessings of his new situation. "Please, Lord, help me not to murmur. You have been so good," he prayed constantly.

With love for God and a desire to help less fortunte people as common ground, Pastor Silva had many good conversations with these other pastors. The great theme of God's love was a topic they never tired of discussing. Several of the men were well acquainted with Seventh-day Adventists. As the conversations progressed, Pastor Silva had a disquieting feeling that though the words were never spoken, his new friends were conveying a message with their eyes and their manner. They seemed to be saying, "Your church teaches that you are the true followers of God. It teaches that you are the chosen people. Yet here you are in prison like the rest of us. How do you explain that?"

Since the words were never enunciated, Pastor Silva could not answer them. He would have told them that the "servant is not greater than his Lord" and that Christ does not promise us freedom from trouble and sorrow. He promises, rather, strength and courage to meet whatever comes.

Nights, though, in spite of the comfort of the mattress, were not as pleasant as Antonio had hoped. They were punctuated by the screams of prisoners being tortured to extract information. As Pastor Silva learned through the prison "grapevine" of the horrors which were taking place along the borders of this country, he became convinced that another power—a lower power, the Prince of Darkness—had laid very firm plans for this sad and beautiful continent, whose people had suffered so long. As he listened to the stories of how diabolically cunning the plotters from other countries were, how skillfully they had programmed the nationals, and how deftly they had turned the latter against the very people who tried to help them, his heart was sick. He wondered and almost despaired as to what the future might hold.

Reading the newspapers, Pastor Silva found that all his fears and apprehensions were justified. He could trace easily the subtle campaign, the devious way in which truth was distorted and the "big lie" made believable.

Then, on Easter weekend, he received proof positive of his suspicions.

"Look!" one of the others had said to him, glancing up from the newspaper. "This article says that all Christians will be allowed to take Good Friday off from work and worship in the church of their choice. Does this mean that religious freedom really will be restored?"

"How marvelous if true," Pastor Silva replied.

His skepticism was well justified. About five o'clock on Good Friday a huge crowd of new prisoners were brought in. Their crime? They were Christians. They had believed the newspaper story. In good faith they had taken the day off from work to attend religious services. The police had checked the rosters of all business places, found the names of the absentees, gone to their homes and churches, arrested them, and imprisoned them.

Knowing the despair and disorientation of new prisoners, Pastor Silva tried, in the minimal contact he was allowed, to speak words of courage to them. "Things are much better here than in other prisons," he told them. "If you must be imprisoned, you could be much worse off than you are."

And so the days passed, one by one. Then about twelve days after the Good Friday incident, without a word of explanation, Pastor Silva was given a clean suit. He immediately recognized it as one of the suits he had left in his apartment. The guards simply handed the clothing to him. Nothing was said. He could find no messages in the suit. If Elena had sent any, they had been confiscated.

His heart began to beat with the now-familiar heavy, thudding stroke. Could it be possible—? When he discovered that his publishing secretary also had received a clean suit, that little sprig of hope burst into full bloom. Later he would learn from Elena that the "friend" who had been working so hard for them had told her that things were nearing fruition. But he and his publishing secretary knew nothing in prison, their nerves becoming so tightly stretched that it seemed as though they would explode. For many months the men had not been in charge of their lives. They felt like pawns in some master chess game.

On Wednesday, April 21, at about four o'clock, twenty days after they had been transferred to the new prison, as they were exercising in the yard, the other prisoners took up a refrain.

"They are calling for the Brazilians. They are calling for the Brazilians."

THE BRAZILIANS! Why, that meant him, Pastor Silva suddenly realized. It meant the publishing secretary. It meant another Brazilian, not an Adventist, but one who had been imprisoned for religious reasons. And it meant a Brazilian whose "crime" had been in the secular category.

Hearts pounding, breath coming in gasps, the four Brazilians ran as fast as they could back to their cells. They were possessed with one overpowering fear—that their absence would not jeopardize whatever new development might be taking place.

But no. The guard gave them an order.

"Get ready to be taken downtown." No other explanation would he give; possibly he knew nothing more, Pastor Silva realized.

As the four men were packed into a car, Pastor Silva and the publishing secretary looked at each other with wide eyes. As the car wended its way, turning at familiar corners, they were aware—with a sense of dazed unreality—that once again they were being taken to the Criminal Investigation Building. Would they be interrogated by the same police inspector who had imprisoned them so summarily? Incredible though it seemed, they were ushered into the all-too-familiar office, but with one change. The inspector was now all smiles.

"Why, I believe that we are coming to the end of this unfortuante incident," he stated smoothly, directing his widest smile at Pastor Silva.

Try as he might, Pastor Silva could not summon a hypocritical smile. But he bowed his head courteously. His manner was impeccable.

"Please sit down," the inspector invited almost jovially.

In a short time another man came in. Dazed, they listened to his bland remarks.

"We are so happy to have heard that your families have secured air tickets for you to fly back to Brazil. We have been waiting for this to happen all these months. It's too bad they didn't try harder to do this," he declared, with never a flicker of the eyes. "Now, if your families will present the tickets to us, proving that you are fully booked for the trip, we will be more than happy to release you," was his next statement.

The tone of his voice was so self-righteous, so studiously affable—as though the government were bestowing an incredible privilege upon these men whom they had imprisoned unfairly and whom they had never charged with crime.

Though he did not permit the slightest emotion to show on his face, inwardly Pastor Silva felt turbulent emotions. Knowing as he did that the tickets had been secured from the Brazilian government about four months previously, and suspecting (which later he would learn was correct) that Elena and the Brazilian airline had called the police dozens of times, asking when they could book a definite flight, it took all his self-control not to reply, not to confront this man with the truth. He sent a swift prayer heavenward.

"Oh, Lord, please help me to hold my tongue," he prayed, knowing that his entire future depended upon his reacting with outward meekness and "going along with the game." He must not, must not give voice to the knowledge that he had.

Sitting there, he remembered something his father had said many times. "In certain kinds of governments, for every five statements, SIX are lies," was his summation. When God was left out, he had told Antonio, another power takes over, a power which deals in lies.

But with total courtesy, in a soft voice, Pastor Silva began asking a few necessary questions.

"We will have to have several documents. Certain steps will have to be taken," he told the smiling inspector. "For instance, who will return our passports to us? When and where will they be returned? We cannot leave without them. To whom should our wives present the tickets?"

No answers seemed forthcoming. All was vague. Would this chance for freedom slip through their fingers through the ineptitude, deliberate or spontaneous, of the officials? Was it another cruel game?

Realizing now that the national government, as represented by the police inspector and the other officials whom he had encountered, would do nothing to make their release easier, would not do even the necessary things unless coerced and prodded, Pastor Silva asked, "May I make a phone call to my wife?"

"You may make a very short call," the inspector agreed grudgingly, his mask of affability slipping a bit.

With a policeman close at his side, Pastor Silva was taken to a nearby room. As he grasped the phone and dialed his house number, his palms were wet with nervous perspiration. In fact, he had broken out in perspiration all over his body. He trembled, knowing that so much was involved for himself and the publishing secretary. This one call was all they would be permitted.

One ring. Two rings. Three rings. Four rings.

He was consumed with panic. Elena MUST be there! She MUST! She MUST answer!

But she didn't. Finally, when he was ready to give up, his hopes crushed, his spirit broken, a voice answered. But it was not Elena's voice. When he recognized the voice of the publishing secretary's wife, his relief was almost too intense to be borne.

"Listen carefully," he told her rapidly. "This is what has happened to us this morning." He recited the meager information that the inspector had given them.

"Work on the tickets. Work on the tickets and the passports," he told her. "It is up to you and Elena. All we can do is pray constantly."

"Time's up," the guard growled.

Antonio hung up in midsentence. Immediately the four Brazilians were hustled back into the car. The now-familiar drive through the streets followed, with Antonio straining his eyes. Could fate be so kind this time as to let him glimpse Elena? It was not to be. With great sadness he reentered the prison.

Immediately he and the others were surrounded by an excited group—the "religious" prisoners.

"What happened? What did they do? Will you be released?" Their questions came thick and fast. Rapidly Pastor Silva told the whole story then concluded, "We will be allowed our freedom, they say, if our wives can secure definite bookings on the airline and can retrieve our passports," he said.

There was a moment of silence. The faces of the others showed joy for him and his friend, but near despair for themselves. "We were arrested long before you were," one of the other pastors said. "We have been in prison for nearly a year, and yet nothing has happened." With bowed heads they turned and walked back to their cells, some of them so discouraged that Pastor Silva never saw them again.

To Pastor Silva sleep that night would be a total impossibility. Even the comfort of the mattress, his most prized possession, did not bring mental peace. Restlessly he tossed as he thought of every eventuality, every complication. Surely he had not been sustained and strengthened so far, only to be crushed now. After much prayer he fell into a light sleep, but was awake long before arising time on Thursday.

At the very first opportunity he and the publishing secretary consulted together. "The man at the police center said that probably I could make another phone call today," Pastor Silva remembered. "So many details need to be worked out. I need desperately to talk with Elena."

Gathering his courage, he approached one of the guards in the corridor, one who had seemed most friendly during these three weeks. He explained his need and made his polite request. He stated that he had been told at the Criminal Investigation Building that he could make a call.

Suddenly the guard started shouting.

"Who do you think you are—asking to make a telephone call! You're a prisoner here just like everybody else. I think I'll give you a good beating! That will teach you how to behave," he continued shouting, now brandishing his club.

Bitterly Pastor Silva said to himself, "So it was yet another lie that I was told. Is there no truth anywhere?"

The rest of the morning dragged by with the two men in a fever of anticipation but with no knowledge of what was taking place on their behalf outside the prison walls. When the wives brought their food, would they receive a message? Would this be the one time the guards would detect the tiny bits of paper, confiscate them, and possibly beat them severely? Worst of all, might they imprison the wives?

With shaking hands, they seized the food from the guard, having watched the iron rods being thrust through it. Ah—here it was! The tiny paper. But as he read it, Pastor Silva's heart sank.

"We have not been able to get definite plane bookings," Elena wrote. "The president of another African country is here making a state visit. He brought so many people with him and is taking so many back that the planes are all full. But don't worry, dearest. Soon we are bound to have the bookings."

It was impossible not to worry.

Antonio and his publishing secretary talked and talked, reviewing every aspect of the situation. During the years they had both worked in this country, they had traveled extensively. They had memorized the schedules of the few planes that landed at the international airport. On Friday there would be a plane to Johannesburg, South Africa, but none would be flying today, Thursday. So they must wait and hope and pray.

But to their shock and disbelief, they were called to the prison commander's office about 4:30 in the afternoon. "Get ready to leave," he told them brusquely. "You are going to be put aboard a plane."

They stared at each other. No plane would leave the airport for other countries until tomorrow. What could this mean? Were they to be shot and their bodies burned, so that no one would ever be able to trace them? With no choice, they decided to cooperate and to conduct themselves as though they were, indeed, being given their freedom.

Sent back to the cell to take care of his meager belongings, Pastor Silva distributed his few possessions to the other men in his cell, including the mattress. He gave as much food as he had left to the national pastor in another cell, and his old clothes also, as he quickly donned the clean jacket and trousers which Elena had sent the day before. He embraced the national pastor with tears and admonitions

160

to remain faithful to God, whatever the cost.

Shaking with anxiety, the two men were taken yet one more time to the Criminal Building. Then ensued a period of much loud talking, arm waving, and arguing between two officials. Heartsick, the two prisoners began to understand that a mistake had indeed been made and that each man blamed the other for it. They had been right. There was no outgoing plane that day.

"Get in the car. You must go back to prison," they were ordered in no uncertain tone of voice.

The walk down the corridor, down the steps, and into the car seemed to Pastor Silva the longest of his life. Freedom had been his—he had touched it with his fingertips. Now it was rudely snatched away again. He felt almost that it would have been better if he had not had his hopes raised so high. The disappointment would not have been so crushing.

But suddenly hope sprang up anew. The car began making turns that he knew would take him by the mission building. "We need to discuss your tickets with your wives," one of the policemen announced.

As the car pulled up to the curb, Elena came running out.

"Antonio, they don't have the tickets ready yet," she exclaimed breathlessly. "There are five of us, you know"—Pastor Silva suddenly remembered that the small adopted daughter of the publishing secretary had not been sent back to Brazil—"and the airline says that tomorrow they have only four seats."

Pastor Silva's mind was working at top speed. "Do you think we could charter a plane to take us across the border?" he asked.

"I don't think we would be allowed to do that, even if a plane were available," Elena answered, all the strain and sorrow of the past six months showing clearly on her face.

"Get in the car!" the guards shouted.

As they pulled into the prison courtyard, Pastor Silva felt for the first time utterly and completely undone. He had thought that he had left this dreary place behind forever; he had given away the small comforts which made his life bearable. Yet here he was back, apparently no nearer freedom than he had been on the first day of his imprisonment. Too well he knew that the government could continue to put up obstacles to his and his friend's release, all the while blandly insisting that they were "trying to effect your freedom."

With dragging footsteps he followed the guard back to the cell, the

161

other prisoners reading the sad story on his face. One by one his possessions were restored to him, silently. Now another long night must be lived through. He tossed and turned. Frustration. Anxiety. Fear. Uncertainty. These were his sleeping companions, and they made for a dreadful night. He could not wait for dawn, yet he was almost afraid for it to come, lest it bring yet another disappointment.

Freedom!

Morning light brought a more welcome emotion. Expectation. He was full of it. His heart lifted. So did the heart of the friend who had endured with him the sufferings of all these months. They were closer than brothers. The two of them waited side by side for the morning food delivery by their wives. The proper time came. But the two women did not come. What was happening?

"Perhaps our freedom is right at hand, this very day, and our wives know that we will not need food," they assured one another, but a growing, anxiety was piercing deep in their chests. Antonio Silva could literally feel the devil sitting on his shoulder whispering to him.

"They didn't bring your food because they have been thrown into prison themselves," the voice beat into his ear. "You don't even know where they are. Probably you will never see Elena again. You will never be free. You will die here in prison. This is what God is asking of you. Do you really still love and worship that kind of cruel tyrant?"

With a great force of will Antonio banished the awful voice in his brain. "Lord, help me!" he cried, and again the Holy Spirit brought a calming wave into his anguished heart.

Twelve o'clock came and went. One o'clock. Two o'clock. Still nothing. No word. No sign.

At three o'clock Pastor Silva happened to glance at his watch. He seemed to glance at it regularly every minute thereafter, and that is how he knew that it was exactly 3:07 p.m. when the front gate of the prison opened, and the government agent who had taken them out of the prison the day before came in sight. As he saw the two men with their faces pressed against the bars, he waved for them to come out and join him. Although it was forbidden at this particular time of day, they opened the door and raced to meet him at the front of the corridor. The commander of the prison appeared.

"You are going to be released," he stated.

It started again—the endless paperwork of many small countries. Then the national pastor came and embraced the two Brazilians, his tears flowing freely. This second emotional farewell further strained their already taut nerves.

Hardly daring to breathe, the two Brazilians followed the agent into the car, which started up with a great clashing of gears and screaming of tires. What was their destination? Finally Pastor Silva risked asking a direct question. The answer came, the sweetest words that he might ever hear in his lifetime. "We are taking you to the airport."

But the two of them could not relax. So much had been left undone from their viewpoint. They were all too aware of the stringent rules of this government and the scrutiny to which their passports would be subjected. Yet they had no passports, and they could not exit without them.

Again summoning his courage, the publishing secretary asked politely, "Could it be that someone has forgotten to return our passports?"

Stony silence was his answer. Both pastors were fearful lest this simple, logical question had so angered the policeman that they might be taken back to prison at once. Then there was conversation between the driver, another soldier, and the agent. One of the passports actually had been left at the Criminal Investigation Building!

"Turn around and go back," the agent commanded.

Pastor Silva wondered if his heart could stand more strain and suspense. Glancing at his friend, he discovered him to be very pale. Both began to pray silently. Each wondered if this incident had been planned, if it had been arranged that a passport be forgotten, that a return trip be made, and thus the two of them would arrive at the airport after the plane had taken off. Of course, in that case, the police could protest that they had tried their best to send them to their own country.

However, at the Criminal Building the agent ran in at top speed and in short order emerged with the passport. Now, for the first time, they allowed themselves to believe that freedom might be at hand. The end of the long ordeal might really be near. As the car moved through one particular intersection, the two pastors gazed at the mission office for what they assumed to be the last time. Pastor Silva could see no sign of life there. He and his friend were afraid to exchange even a word. "Lord, please let Elena and my friend's family be at the airport. Please don't let anything delay them. Please don't let anything go wrong," Antonio petitioned.

When the car pulled up to the airport after what had seemed an endless time span, the agent firmly ordered them to enter by a special door, where they would have no contact with other passengers. Quickly they were hustled into a small room. They were kept incommunicado.

Feeling in his pockets, Pastor Silva found a small amount of money. Elena had managed to get it to him in the food so that he would not be entirely penniless.

"This money will do me no good outside this country," he told the agent. "I am happy to make you a present of it." The agent seized it eagerly, scant though it was.

Now Pastor Silva's agile brain began clicking away again, formulating plans and ideas and inventorying what was probably going on in the main section of the airport. He reasoned that Elena would have had to bring with her all their possessions which she could not bear to leave behind, whatever clothes they still owned and a few keepsakes. This might mean that her luggage would be overweight. He was aware of the enormous fee placed on overweight luggage in that airport. If Elena did not have enough money, then they would not be able to leave. Dare he mention the problem to the agent? He gathered his courage. In his most courteous manner he spoke.

"Sir," he said, "my wife will probably have quite a lot of luggage. But I have none. Do you think it could be arranged for some of the luggage to be put on my ticket?" (As it turned out, Elena had almost nothing, but at that point he could not know this.)

The agent seemed to indicate by a few guttural murmurs that perhaps this could be done. But Pastor Silva's heart was still not at ease. He had not yet seen Elena and the others. He could not allow himself to be put on a plane unless he was first sure that she and the others were coming or were already on board. He had been tricked so many times and had believed so many promises only to learn in sorrow and anguish that he had been deceived. This time he must be totally sure.

"Please," he spoke to the agent again, with all his pent-up emotion showing in his face, "please take me to the area where I think my wife will be checking in. Surely you must understand that I need to have a glimpse of her."

After a moment of silence, which stretched into a small eternity, the agent agreed. "I will take both of you," he answered.

Then, for the first time in six months, the two of them were together in the midst of free people. To their enormous surprise, some of the church members were in the airport, a most unusual occurrence, since for some time only passengers had been allowed there.

"Pastor Silva! Pastor Silva! one or two of them called to him softly. Then they crowded around, patting him and shaking his hands. Torn now with emotion and nervousness, he glanced about the airport, his eyes searching, searching, even as he shook hands and murmured greetings, conscious of his rather rough appearance.

THEN HE SAW HER! Elena was there! The others were there! Such a rush of joy filled his heart that he could hardly contain it. He would never know until later all that this magnificent woman had done to bring this day about. For now, he knew only that God was good.

"Now come back to the room with me," the agent ordered roughly, This time Pastor Silva and the publishing secretary walked on winged feet. Their wives were in the airport. They were checking in for the flight. No longer did it matter that the men must be confined in this room until they boarded the plane. Nothing mattered now except the glorious fact of near freedom and reunion.

Then the agent gave the two men their passports and certain other documents which had been taken from them so many months before on that terrible Friday. The money which they had had in their pockets at the time of their arrest was not returned. Pastor Silva remembered with a wry smile that the publishing secretary had been carrying a large amount. Someone obviously had "liberated" it.

But he was not fully free of concern yet. Suddenly it came to his mind that he had heard a disquieting rumor. He had been told by other prisoners that Europeans leaving the country were often ordered at the airport to strip off all their clothes so that the police could be completely certain that they were not smuggling anything out. Often insulting and rude remarks were made. Sometimes women were not treated with respect. Fearfully he wondered if this might happen to Elena. He was in no position to offer her his protection. His only recourse was as usual the quick, silent petition to God for help and courage and peace of mind.

Suddenly the door opened—and there was Elena! Since she was being expelled from the country, she had not been ordered to disrobe. She had now passed through passport control and customs. Nothing stood in the way of their embarkation. Following behind her was the wife of the publishing secretary with her little girl. The two couples were so overcome by the emotion of their reunion that they could communicate only in embraces and broken whispers. After so many months of strain, they were almost drained of any ability to react.

Behind all the joy was the still-present concern. The plane should have departed at 4:40 p.m., and now it was 6 o'clock. They began to think of everything that could go wrong. They did not share these thoughts with one another lest in the very communicating they bring the trouble to pass.

Then the door opened once more. They were ordered to walk out to the runway and board the plane. It was just sundown—sundown on another Friday, but how different from that Friday in October. Pastor Silva thought that he had never seen the sky so beautiful, with some of the blue still showing among the rose and mauve and gold and the spectacular cloud formations. The devoted church members who had braved the wrath of their government in order to catch a last glimpse of their beloved leaders waved and waved from the observation deck at the top of the airport.

Pastor Silva agonized over leaving them, those for whom he had come to this country, for whom he had labored, and whom he had grown to love. He must make some kind of gesture. He was carrying his briefcase, which Elena had brought. He set it down on the runway, turned, bowed low to the believers, then waved and waved. His eyes were wet. In spite of all he had endured, he did not want to be separated from "his people."

So many hopes, plans, goals, and desires were now dead. This would be, Pastor Silva knew, an enormous setback to the work of God in this needy country. He continued to wonder if he had made any mistakes which had brought the situation to this point, as he had so often wondered through the prison months.

As for himself and Elena, they had nothing in the world but two small suitcases and two briefcases. All their household possessions, he would learn, had been sold to take care of everyday expenses and to buy food for him in prison. They were starting all over again at the bottom of the material ladder. But how unimportant that seemed! How little anything mattered except God and being together again.

He found, though, that he was unable yet to regard himself as a full-fledged human being among other free human beings. So long used to regimentation and to the denial of human dignity, he broke out in cold perspiration as he ascended the steps of the plane, following Elena. He did not know how to act. He was afraid he would betray his uncertainty by some foolish gesture, some unintelligent action.

The smiling stewardess greeted them at the door of the plane. Not by a flicker of an eyelash did she indicate that his somewhat shaggy appearance was anything out of the ordinary. Well, he said to himself, everyone is used to young people with long, scraggly hair and blue jeans; so that situation is working for my benefit just now. Nonetheless, he shrank from what he thought were curious glances from the other passengers. If they knew that he had just been released after six months in prison, would they demand that he not be allowed on the plane? Would the others fear him, thinking that a criminal was in their midst?

But now they were walking down the aisle, directed to seats by another stewardess. The familiar routine came back to him, the settling in the seat, the buckling of the seat belt, but most of all, by his side, his dear, dear Elena. In his moments of darkest despair he had thought that he would never again travel with her—by air, or any other way.

He clasped her hand tightly. In his eyes Elena could see all that he longed to say and would say in the future. For now, though, he could not talk.

All the passengers were on the plane. The door slammed shut. Then a final terror struck Antonio. He remembered several prisoners who had told him that they had actually been on planes, ready to fly out, when police had halted the takeoff of the plane, had come aboard, and dragged them back to prison. The thought of one man in particular suddenly invaded his mind. This man had been on a plane with his wife and children. He had been dragged off. When he was thrown back into the cell, for four or five days he had stood gazing at the wall, completely catatonic, unable to deal with the monstrous reality.

Would this—could this—happen to him? Antonio felt that if it did, his heart, overburdened as it was, might literally explode with grief.

He clasped Elena's hand ever more tightly.

Now the motors were revving up. They roared with increasing power. The plane began to vibrate. Slowly the wheels began to move. Slowly—so slowly, it seemed to him, the huge jet taxied out onto the long runway and sat at the end for a moment. Then, as he had so often dreamed in the packed and reeking cell, in a burst of unrestrained speed the plane raced down the runway and literally leaped into the sky, into the beautiful, glorious sunset, into the rose and gold and mauve, into the drifting, scudding, snow-white clouds, into God's glorious heaven, into the rest of his life.

He was free.

He was free.

He was free.

Epilogue

During the short flight to Johannesburg, South Africa, Pastor Silva and his friend discovered that their passports had been stamped "Expelled" and their tickets carried the words, "Deported." This caused considerable concern among the two couples, for the men had no visas for South Africa. They now had passports indicating that they were undesirables. They had no World Health Cards with the required vaccinations listed. Would they be admitted? The plane for South America would not leave until midnight on Saturday. What would they do if they were refused entry? They could not even bear to think that they might even be sent back.

Elena's faith never wavered. She told Antonio some of the things she had done to secure the tickets and some of what she had done to secure his release. She told him that all their furniture was gone. Some she had sold, but some she had given to church members; some she had had to leave standing in the little apartment they had loved. At times she had not had enough to eat, as he had suspected. When he asked her how much food was left in their kitchen, she replied, "Half a kilo of rice—nothing more." And she had no money. God had rescued them just in time. His books, in spite of everything, she had managed to send back to Brazil.

All through the preparations for landing in Johannesburg the four became more and more tense. Only one more hurdle to cross. As they disembarked, immediately they recognized their old friend, a Brazilian compatriot, now on the staff of the General Conference. He was waving delightedly from the top of the observation post on the airport. Pastor Silva shouted to him, "No visa!" Pastor S——— shouted back, "Arrangements made!" And they were. The five, including the little girl, were sent on through to the main lobby, free as birds.

During the evening, phone calls were made to Brazil and to the United States, informing all of the wonderful news. Pastor Silva was so keyed up, so tense, that he could not sleep in the nice hotel to which he and Elena and the others were taken. He had thought, through all those horrifying months, that if he could just be free, all would be perfect. But his overstrained nerves would give him no peace. During the next day he was rushed from church to church, to say a few words and to talk to all the people who had prayed for his release.

At one of the churches he tried to preach, but the words would not come easily. He could not relax. Nothing seemed real. Was this just a dream? Would he wake up in the packed cell? Had his mind shattered, as he had so often feared that it might?

Then the long flight to South America, the joyful reunion at the airport with all the family members and scores and scores of friends. When Pastor Silva embraced Maria and Lucila, and then his mother and father, and then Elena's parents, his cup of joy was too full to contain more. During the drive to Elena's parents' home, he resolved that the first thing he would do upon entering the house was to gather all the family members and kneel and express his fervent thanks to God.

The trip was a blur. He remembered almost nothing. Hours later, he awoke, fully clothed, on a bed, his physical fatigue having been so great that he had collapsed.

Pastor Silva steadfastly refused to resume his life with his family until he could receive a clean bill of health from a physician. On Monday he started his physical examinations and tests, the specter of leprosy, tuberculosis, or other dread diseases always in his mind. During the examination the physician looked very grave. He announced that Antonio's liver seemed much inflamed. This could have proven to be a very serious matter, but the medication he was given eventually cured the problem. One physical disorder which has never cleared up, however, are black retinal dots which weave from side to side in his line of vision. Otherwise, he was pronounced clear of any diseases.

Then Antonio's soul slipped into a dark night. He could not bear to be in crowds of people. He could not endure the constant questioning, the incessant urging to describe his imprisonment. It seemed to him that his entire body was one raw, exposed nerve, with all the sights and sounds of life rubbing on it like salt.

When he would accept a preaching appointment during his three months' medical leave, it took such a fearful toll that he wondered if he could endure it. He endeavored to shake hands with members at the door of the churches, a practice he had always delighted in doing, but now, as one by one they told him how they had prayed for him, he began to feel that it was all a kind of mockery. The terrible thought entered his mind that perhaps it would have been better for him to die in the packed cell than to have this overwhelming feeling of helplessness, this panic, this constant anxiety.

At first he tried to hide his desperate condition from Elena. But she was too emotionally close to him not to understand. When at last he voiced his fears, her warm reassurance was a bulwark. She assured him that his psychological state was predictable and normal, considering what he had been through. The human spirit can endure only so much.

The time came for him to assume the pastorship of the church which Elena had described while he was in the packed cell. But he was still in despair. His mind and body seemed devastated. It seemed improbable that he could ever work again. He feared that he would be nothing but a burden to Elena. When his mother-in-law asked him to drive her on an errand in the car, it took every ounce of willpower and self-control for him to take the wheel. He was soaked with perspiration when he returned to the house.

When the move to the lovely city was accomplished, he found that the church had been without a pastor for some time. The members were very hungry for spiritual leadership. He found it difficult to concentrate long enough to prepare new sermons. So he took his Bible, the book which had sustained him through the imprisonment, and began to call on his members, one by one, reading and studying the Bible with them. As the days went by, little by little he began to feel his old bouyancy of spirit returning. He felt the old optimism, the strength and leadership which were so much a part of his nature. He thanked God many times a day as his life began to take on new and glorious dimensions. In working for others he worked out his own rehabilitation, both physically and emotionally.

At present Pastor Silva is back in administrative work, after having pastored that church for two years. His executive skills were so badly needed in South America that when the call came to reenter administration, he felt not only that the Lord was calling him, but that he was ready to answer the call to a leadership role. Maria and Lucila are in a large Seventh-day Adventist boarding school and doing very well. The four Silvas are reunited on every holiday and during the summers. Antonio and Elena are again a team, she working along with him, as always, making his life her life.

When the Euro-Africa Division asked Pastor and Mrs. Silva to make a list of all the material possessions that they had lost, so that restitution could be made, they began a list, but they could not finish it. They were so overwhelmed with gratitude to God for Antonio's deliverance that they sent back this word: "If you will allow us the small sum of ——— we will be more than satisfied."

The story would not be complete without a few more words about that valiant and intrepid woman, Elena Silva. Had Pastor Silva, during his imprisonment, known of all her activities, he would indeed have been beside himself! She never gave up hope. She never lost her spirit. When the treasurer of the mission had to leave precipitously, he put the keys of the treasury, the accounting books, and all of the office cash in Elena's hands. With that money in her possession she was in severe danger of being imprisoned herself.

Moreover, since the incident that sparked the entire chain of imprisonments was the enrolling of people in the Bible Correspondence School, early in his imprisonment Pastor Silva had sent a message on one of the scraps of paper instructing Elena to close down the school. In fact, he asked her not even to enter the office area where the school had been conducted, lest this small act bring suspicion on her. He reasoned that if the police should make a surprise raid on the mission office and find her in that area of the building, they would need no further excuse to imprison her also.

Elena read his warnings. She certainly meant to be an obedient wife, as always. But when the secretary of the school had to make her escape out of the country, leaving two or three thousand active enrollments, Elena was the only one left who knew how to operate this soul-winning agency. So she evolved the plan of entering the second floor office after dark, closing the windows and covering them, and working by the light of a single candle.

She also figured out a way to mail the lessons back to the students without arousing undue suspicion. Each morning she would call some Adventist members whom she knew to be completely loyal and trustworthy. To them she would give the lessons and postage money, instructing them to take the lessons each day to a different branch post office. In this way no single postal inspector saw the large piles every day. As a further precaution, she sent the lessons back in plain envelopes carrying no return address. Nonetheless, had Antonio been aware of her determination to keep sending the lessons as long as possible, he would probably not have slept even the little that he did in prison.

Moreover, every day Elena's nerves were bombarded with rumors ("All prisoners will be shot today") and advice ("You must leave this country immediately") and ("You can do your husband no good, and you have to think of your girls") and danger in the streets ("Any white woman who ventures onto the streets will be assaulted"). She too had had very little sleep for the six months of Antonio's imprisonment. For the first few months she had the entire care of the two girls. She had to secure food one way or another. She had to act as a tower of strength in calming their fears, never showing her own fear, which she could not help feeling. Then she was called upon to send her two children back to Brazil by themselves. At the airport she shed no tears lest they cling to her and refuse to leave.

Probably the worst stress she had to endure on a regular basis was the twice-weekly trip to the courtyard. Her glimpses of Antonio showed him to be steadily deteriorating physically. As she contemplated the conditions under which he was being held—though mercifully she could not know all—she prayed constantly that his nerves and spirit would be made equal to the unspeakable horror.

On her most important days of each week, Sundays and Thursdays, she had to get permission to enter the prison yard for each "visit"— surely an irony. Early in the morning she went to the prison gate and stood in line under the broiling tropical sun, among people of all walks of life, among criminals and drug addicts and other dregs of society, until about two o'clock in the afternoon. Her white skin marked her as an enemy. But she never failed Antonio.

Much of her time was spent in scouring the city for food. The country had almost ground to a halt under the inefficiency and corruption of the new government. This made her responsibilities almost impossible.

Finally she was the only person left in charge of the mission. She felt that she must keep it open as long as possible, for a steady stream of national believers came to her for advice and counsel. She was sadly aware that unless the attitude of the government changed, many of her dear national friends might spend the rest of their lives in prison. Every day she prayed for strength for just that one day. She prayed for superhuman wisdom.

Always her most important and overriding task was exploring every possible avenue that could lead to Antonio's release. She went from one government office to another, tirelessly, until her valiant person was rather well known. She suffered constant rebuffs, insults, and discouragements, but she continued to wage her campaign. Over and over she was put off with promises such as "We will study his case." At first she believed these promises; later she came to know that they were meaningless.

Every Sabbath morning, every Sunday and Wednesday evening, she (and the two girls until they went back to Brazil) walked, carrying their Bibles and hymnals to the church for the meetings. This meant ten blocks of walking in a city where constant gunfire was carried on in the streets and where foreigners had been declared fair game. She would not have taken the risk except for the fact that she was the only remaining link with church leadership—she and her valiant friend, the publishing secretary's wife—and the national believers clung to them like drowning men to a straw. Often she had to do the preaching herself. She encouraged the members to continue to attend, for their spiritual strength would depend on their mutual caring and fellowship.

As the expatriate missionaries went back to their home countries, family by family, Elena, now in charge of the treasury, had to pay their salaries so that they could purchase their air tickets. In addition, she had to decide how best to use the money which some of the Portuguese laymen gave her before they, too, escaped, since they could take no money with them.

* * * * *

In the three dark months following Antonio's release, Elena was always by his side, always encouraging him, always certain that the Lord would restore him to full health and former capabilities.

When Pastor Silva is asked these days to tell some of his experiences, though he prefers not to dwell on them, he always ends his story this way:

"Next to our heavenly Father, my dear companion deserves my greatest praise for her courage, loyalty, love, patience, faith, and coolness. I thank the Lord for giving her to me; He could have given me no greater blessing."